MEMORABLE DESCRIPTION OF THE EAST INDIAN VOYAGE

1618-1625

MEMORABLE DESCRIPTION OF THE EAST INDIAN VOYAGE

1618-1625

WILLEM YSBRANTSZ BONTEKOE

TRANSLATED FROM THE DUTCH BY

C. B. BODDE-HODGKINSON
PIETER GEYL

WITH AN INTRODUCTION AND NOTES BY

PIETER GEYL

GYAN

Published by

Gyan Publishing House
5, Ansari Road
Daryaganj, New Delhi-110002
Phone: 011-47034999, 9811692060
E-mail: books@gyanbooks.com

Distribution Network
gyanbooks.com
India, USA, Canada, UK, Australia, France

ISBN : 978-81-212-3777-2 (PB)
First Published, London, 1929

2nd Impression 2020

Printed at: Gyan Press, Delhi.

Memorable Description of the East Indian Voyage
Author: Willem Ysbrantsz Bontekoe

THE BROADWAY TRAVELLERS

EDITED BY SIR E. DENISON ROSS
AND EILEEN POWER

WILLEM YSBRANTSZ BONTEKOE

MEMORABLE DESCRIPTION OF THE EAST INDIAN VOYAGE

1618—25

Translated from the Dutch by

MRS. C. B. BODDE-HODGKINSON AND PIETER GEYL, Lit.D. (Leyden), Professor of Dutch History and Institutions in the University of London

with an Introduction and Notes by

PROFESSOR GEYL

Published by

GEORGE ROUTLEDGE & SONS, LTD.

BROADWAY HOUSE, CARTER LANE, LONDON

LIST OF ILLUSTRATIONS

PLATE		PAGE
I.	*Title Page, edition of* 1646 . . .	*Frontispiece*
II.	*Willem Ysbrantsz Bonte-Koe Van Hoorn* . . .	18
III.	" *They danced and capered and rejoiced right merrily* " .	36
IV.	*The Shipwreck*	42
V.	" *Seeing no land yet came in sight, we resolved to take them in* "	50
VI.	" *There stood a great company of the inhabitants chattering most vehemently amongst themselves* " . .	60
VII.	" *There came running from out of the woods two or three hundred men* "	64
VIII.	" *Therefore I fell on my knees and prayed to God* " . .	70
IX.	" *The hurricane continued about six or eight glasses* " .	132
X.	" *We were busied every day to repair our damage* " . .	138

JOURNAL

OR

MEMORABLE DESCRIPTION

OF THE

EAST INDIAN VOYAGE OF WILLEM YSBRANTZ BONTEKOE OF HOORN,

Comprehending many wonderful and perilous happenings experienced therein;

Begun on the 18th of December, 1618, and completed on the 16th November, 1625.

At Hoorn, Printed by Isaac Willemsz,

For Jan Jansz Deutel, Book-seller in the East Street, in Biestkins Testament;

Anno 1646.

INTRODUCTION

Bontekoe's East Indian Voyage was one of the most popular of the numerous adventure books in which the Dutch seventeenth century public delighted. It appeared at Hoorn in 1646, more than twenty years after the events related; in the next few years over a dozen piratical editions were brought out in various Dutch towns. All through the seventeenth and eighteenth centuries it continued to be reprinted. Bontekoe's name became part of the Dutch language, and "een reis van Bontekoe" is still a common expression to denote a journey with more than its due share of accidents.

Yet it is only to the discernment and perseverance of Jan Jansz. Deutel, printer at Hoorn, that we owe the preservation of the Captain's great story at all. He himself, as Deutel relates in his Dedication to their Honours, the Directors of the Hoorn Chamber of the East India Company, "already seemed to have vowed it to oblivion". Deutel, who writes with a portentous solemnity, and in an elaborately classicist style, contrasting curiously with Bontekoe's downright simplicity, assures his patrons, after a dissertation on patriotism in general, that he has always been keen to make known to the world the deeds accomplished by natives of the town of Hoorn. When he was permitted to read Captain Bontekoe's manuscript he at once, in spite of the Captain's modest depreciation of his own work,

> "found it to be worthy to remain in eternal remembrance with us and our descendants. Accordingly I begged of him that he would let me print it, but he was not inclined thereto, partly because the events were almost forgotten and grown old by time, partly because he had not described them in such a style as was, in his opinion, suitable to be printed. Finally, after much amicable entreaty and insistence of some of his good friends, did he give his consent."

Indeed, Bontekoe's relation betrays the inexperienced author on every page. The art of connecting his sentences, of avoiding repetitions, of delicately indicating that unimportant events later on will acquire significance, the technique of the story-teller, in short, was unknown to the man who knew all there was to be known about the art of conducting a ship and a ship's company through the awful difficulties and perils of an East Indian voyage. There are many passages in the book where one is almost tempted to take the pen from the worthy Captain's clumsy hand and tell his story for him in an amended form. There are other passages where one would give anything to be able to interview him so as to get hold of the really interesting details which he forgot to set down. Sometimes again he is so obscure as to leave one guessing at his precise meaning.

And yet! how very grateful should we be to Mr. Deutel not only for having persuaded the ageing Captain to let his manuscript be published, but for having refrained from doing any of the things which we may safely wish we could do, but which he undoubtedly could have done, and would have spoilt a lovely book in doing them. How cordially do we forgive the pedantry of his own Dedication and Preface since he has allowed Bontekoe to speak to us in his homely language uncensored.

For with all his shortcomings as an author Bontekoe was himself by far the best possible narrator of his stupendous labours and adventures. If his book has become famous it is not only on account of the matter it has to relate. As to that, once more Deutel, who was certainly not a bad judge of the work he published, will tell us why it made such an instantaneous, and such a lasting, appeal.

"'Tis just what you want", he assures the Reader in his Preface. "Here you will find no trifling, nor dreams, nor fabulous imaginings. Nor was this description made on hearsay,—no, it is based on personal experience, relating what miracles God performed by the author himself and those who were with him. For who shall not greatly marvel when reading how a man of that human kind who come so often to a sudden end—through so much peril and adversity, indeed through stresses in which to hope for any escape appeared to be like despairing, was by the Lord's mercy brought to a place of safety!"

That was, and always will be, the chief attraction of the book: the spectacle of a human being battling against elemental forces, at tremendous odds, tenaciously holding on to dear life, and coming safely through in the end.

But it would not be so attractive, nor so moving, if Bontekoe, by the manner of his telling the story, did not reveal his own personality so completely and so engagingly. He was himself pervaded with that sense of the miraculous that communicates itself to his readers, he was sensitive both to the tragedy of disaster and to the goodness of God apparent in escape. And so he does not merely describe the external events—although he does describe them to some purpose when they have gripped his attention—but he continually notes, with the most disarming sincerity and absence of display, his own mental reactions to them.

No doubt he wants us to know that he was in the right in all his conflicts with those intolerable persons, the "Merchants", who represented on his ship the interests and the authority of his and their "Lords and Masters", the Directors of the Company. But how refreshing to hear him confess to "fear and trembling" whenever the occasion is such that anybody except professional heroes would succumb to human weakness of that kind. Of professional heroism there is remarkably little to be found in the book.

Neither in the encounters with the "Specks", nor in the miserable "war" made on the unfortunate Chinese, least of all perhaps in the terrible story of the fire, is there anything spectacular for Dutch chauvinism to feast its eyes on. Bontekoe never tries to embellish. And how charmingly he pictures himself in his relations with the men. He never pretends that his word was law with them. In fact, however pleasant the spectacle of the Captain of an East-Indiaman ruling his crew with "gentle words", and inviting their opinion before giving orders, there are occasions when by his own account Bontekoe clearly appears as somewhat deficient in strength and decision.

At the same time, it should be remembered that the system of Councils, which pervaded the whole service of the Company as it did the government of the Dutch Republic, encouraged methods of deliberation and consultation rather than of command. In a general way it may be said that the Dutch as a nation were, and are, more easily led than driven, and although I imagine that Bontekoe might on one or two occasions have been a little firmer, on the whole he seems to me in this respect to have been truly typical of the splendid class of men to which he belonged.

The important thing is that before reading very long one begins to see Bontekoe as a living man, and a lovable man at that. The sense of human contact which his simple narrative conveys so strongly heightens the interest in his adventures. Admiration for the superhuman endurance of that very human person grows upon one as his misfortunes accumulate without breaking his cheerful determination to try all the resources of his technical skill and inventiveness before giving himself up for lost. Does it not amount to saying that Bontekoe possessed at least one quality of the born story-teller in a very high degree? And, indeed, however faulty his technique, it does not obscure that quality, which still works its spell triumphantly with countless readers.

Apart from the year of his birth—1587—hardly anything is known about Willem Ysbrantsz(oon) Bontekoe except what may be learnt from his journal. The second name is, of course, a patronymic, indicating that his father's Christian name was Ysbrant. It will be observed in the book that the use of patronymics was still general in early seventeenth century Holland. Third names—that is, family names—were far less common. Bontekoe's own name, which means Piebald Cow, was pretty certainly derived from a sign decorating his father's house at Hoorn; it may have been a shop or an inn. He says himself, in the course of his book, that he had never been in the Indies before he went there on this voyage in command of the ill-fated *Nieuw-Hoorn*. Probably he never went again.

When he sailed from the Texel on 18th December, 1618, it was just over twenty-one years since Cornelis de Houtman had fallen into that port after having accomplished the first Dutch voyage round the Cape of Good Hope. The success of De Houtman's expedition had caused a number of companies for trading in the East to be formed in various towns of Holland and Zeeland. From 1598 to 1601 no less than fourteen fleets totalling sixty-five ships went from the Netherlands to the Indies, most of them to Java and the Moluccas, to ship pepper and spices. Some of these companies made enormous profits, but it was plain to everybody that their competition and rivalry endangered the whole of this new-born trade. Both to preserve the cheapness of the native markets and to protect the new position against the Portuguese, combination was urgently required. The government of the Dutch Republic took a hand, to bring the interested parties together. The Portuguese, whose monopoly in the Eastern world was so suddenly invaded had been, since 1580, the subjects of the King of Spain and as such at war with the United Provinces, whose independence the King of Spain still was a long way from recognising. To attack the Portuguese colonies was therefore to attack the enemy in one of the sources of his wealth, and when in 1602, after negotiations under the conduct of the "Advocate" Oldenbarnevelt himself, the trading Companies were amalgamated, the States-General granted to the United Dutch East India Company a monopoly preventing all other Dutchmen from trading between the Cape of Good Hope and Cape Magelhaes and at the same time delegated to it sovereign powers, which made it into an extremely powerful body for attack and conquest in the area of its monopoly.

The organisation of the Company presented clear evidence of its having sprung from the amalgamation of earlier and independent bodies. It consisted of several "Chambers", having their seats in the various trading towns which had taken part in the early voyages. The Amsterdam Chamber was the principal one, there was one in Zeeland, one in the Maas district (Rotterdam and Delft), and one in the Zuiderzee region (Hoorn and Enkhuizen). Hoorn in the sixteenth and early seventeenth centuries was a busy shipping centre. Later, with the increasing draft of seagoing vessels, the shallowness of the Zuiderzee became an obstacle of ever more serious importance, until the town became the quiet rural market and fishing port which it is to-day.

In the first years of its existence, the Company's fleets repeatedly attacked all the main strongholds of the Portuguese colonial system, Mozambique, Goa, Malacca, but all these attacks failed, and it was only on the Moluccas, coveted because only there were the precious spices grown, that the Dutch succeeded, by dint of hard fighting, in getting a foothold. On several of the islands, the Portuguese, who here had the direct support of the Spaniards from the Philippines were ousted, Dutch fortresses were built, and the populations compelled to trade only with the Dutch, and on their terms. The Dutch did not only export the spices. They had managed to obtain a footing on the Coromandel coast and from there imported the widely-famed cloths into the Archipelago. It was their ambition to eliminate all other traders, native and European, and acquire a carrying monopoly in the Eastern world such as they already possessed in Europe.

They were still far removed from that ideal. At Bantam, the great commercial centre of the Archipelago, which had been their first objective because the Portuguese had no fortified post there, or near it, they still had to be content with a competitive position. And it was not only the Portuguese and the Indians themselves who competed. In the wake of the Dutch expeditions the English had followed, and their activities, both in the Moluccas, and in Java, caused not a little anxiety and resentment to the Dutch.

The Moluccas, precious in themselves, were too remote to serve as a centre from which to control a trading movement that already embraced the Archipelago and the Indian mainland and stretched out feelers towards China and Japan. In 1610, the Directors, realising the need for a unified and continuous command in the area of their monopoly, had instituted the office of a Governor-General, who was to be assisted by a Council. But this was an itinerant government. For several years the Governor-General and Council travelled up and down between the Moluccas and Bantam; where they could be said to be on their own territory only when they were on board ship. The need for a general *rendezvous*, a seat for the central authority, became pressing.

When Bontekoe set sail from the Texel, in December, 1618, momentous events were just taking place in the Indies. In that same year Jan Pieterszoon Coen, the most illustrious son of Bontekoe's native town, Hoorn, had received his appointment as Governor-General. He was a man of vision and determination, ruthless in his dealings with the Indian peoples, and little inclined to allow considerations of European politics to stand in the way of a struggle with the English, whose intrusion in the Archipelago he looked upon as the most serious menace to the future of the Dutch Company. In the summer of 1618 he began building a fortress at

Jacatra, a vassal town of Bantam, a little more to the East on the North coast of Java, as "a provisional *rendezvous*". An open rupture with Bantam and the English simultaneously allowed him, a few months later, to turn the provisional into the permanent. Jacatra was destroyed and Batavia founded on its ruins. Bantam was blockaded and its trade paralysed. The English were chased out of the Archipelago. When Bontekoe arrives at Batavia in December, 1619, and placidly calls it by that name without a word of comment, seven months had not elapsed since the old Jacatra was wiped off the map. Politics are no concern of our author. He only tells us what the Governor-General had to say about his adventures, and soon is busy carrying stone for the powerful castle that was now constructed at Batavia.

The English had been worsted in Asia, but in Europe the States-General had to humour them, and so Coen, to his intense disgust, soon learnt that they had to be admitted to a share in the Indian trade and that friendly co-operation had to be attempted with them in accordance with an arrangement concluded at London between the English and the Dutch Companies. It was an arrangement that soon broke down under the suspicion and ill-will of the men who were to carry it out, and the real superiority of the Dutch Company's resources as well as its strategical position, in consequence of Coen's policy, explains why the breakdown left it in command of the situation. Bontekoe has occasion to mention English ships as acting jointly with Dutch fleets, near the Philippines and off Macao. In fact the English were never able to pull much weight in the expeditions which were in the next few years organized by Coen's restless energy, and the instruction given to the Dutch commanders made it clear that English assistance was not really desired at Batavia.[1] The " Amboyna Massacre ", to which there is no direct reference in Bontekoe's pages, but of which distant echoes may be heard[2], was the tragic conclusion of the co-operation comedy.

After some years of rather humdrum service in the Archipelago Bontekoe was employed on one of those expeditions by which Coen hoped to extend the Company's trade, namely that which was sent in April, 1622, to attack the Portuguese fortress of Macao and to open up trade with China. The expedition, led by Cornelis Reyertsz, was a dismal failure. The attempt against Macao was given up after some operations that were severely censured by Bontekoe in a letter to Coen[3]. No match for the Dutch at sea, the Portuguese always offered stubborn resistance against attacks on land. Later on, under the Governor-General Van Diemen and Maetsuycker, the conquest of Ceylon, of Malacca, Negapatam and the Malabar Coast, was to prove a very arduous and costly business. And Reyertsz was hardly more successful against the Chinese than he had been against the Portuguese. He came with the offer of an amicable treaty of commerce. The Chinese, however, happened to be in a far from friendly mood towards foreigners, as a result of friction with the Portuguese. Moreover, the Dutch asked for much more than permission to trade for themselves. They wanted to direct a blow against their enemies and to interrupt the profitable trade which the Portuguese from Macao and Malacca, and the Spaniards from Manilla, were still carrying on with China. They presumed to ask that no junks should trade except with their permits. And before entering into conversations with the Chinese authorities at all, Reyertsz occupied Pehu, in the Pescadores (11th July, 1622), which was Chinese territory, and fitted out the island as a naval base, building a fort on the south-western extremity. This angered the Chinese, and the proposals addressed to the authorities of the Amoy District—" the river of Chinchu " having been selected as the likeliest Chinese harbour—were met only with the urgent demand that they should evacuate Pehu. 2nd October, 1622, Reyertsz and his Council decided to make war on the Chinese, to see if thus they might not be brought to change their minds. Now began a futile and degrading " war ", in which a fleet of never more than a dozen ships manned by 1,000 or 1,200 men tried to harass the immense and impassive empire of China, by marauding expeditions on a few miles of coast and by burning a few villages and a few score of junks. It was made more repulsive by the demand of the authorities at Batavia for Chinese captives. Coen, his imagination aflame with the vision of a populous Batavia, that would feed trade and make remittances of money from home superfluous, was especially keen and largely responsible for the slave-raiding policy that resulted.

Bontekoe gives the facts stoically, and it is instructive to see a man, as humane as he is where his own kind is concerned, so insensitive to the sufferings of an alien race. On the one hand his laconic statement that the captives were " sold " at Batavia is apt to give a wrong impression. They were distributed among the principal Chinese already settled there, who undertook to pay a ransom of 60 reals of eight per head for them, in fifteen monthly instalments. After that they were apparently on the same footing as other Chinese colonists.[1] It was a system of enforced settlement, and really a sincere compliment to the docility and industriousness of the Chinese. Yet on the other hand, the full horror of these proceedings does not appear in Bontekoe's account of them. Not many of the 1,400 captives mentioned by him as working on the Pescadores ever reached Batavia, whether to be sold or indentured.

One hundred and eighty, transferred to the *Haerlem* from the *Groningen*, seem to have arrived all right. But of 1,150, waiting on the Pescadores, so many died that in September, 1623, only 571 were left to be shipped to Batavia, and of these in January, 1624, no more than thirty-three disembarked alive.

Reyertsz had soon come to see that nothing could be effected by the methods adopted. The forces at his disposal were too small to make any impression on the Chinese rulers, except that the outrages committed raised their hatred and resentment. It was only his successor in the command of the expedition, however, Dr. Sonck, who took charge in August, 1624, when Bontekoe was already back at Batavia, who succeeded in making the Governor-General (De Carpentier) consent to a change of policy.

"Our proceedings on the coast of China", Sonck wrote, "have so embittered the whole of China against us that we are looked upon as no better than murderers, tyrants and pirates. Our dealings with the Chinese have indeed been very hard and cruel, and in my opinion such that the desired trade could never be obtained by them.

"It would be better had we never been on the coast of China, and I wish that Your Honours, before the departure from Batavia of the Commander Reyertsz, had been accurately informed of the power and customs of the Chinese as well as of the conditions of the country. In that case perhaps the entire empire of China, and the Emperor himself, would not have been disposed against us with hostility and revenge. Now these and many other inconveniences and misfortunes will first, if possible, have to be in the aptest way eliminated, before the Company will be able to obtain the long desired fruits of that over-excellent Chinese trade."

The Pescadores were at once evacuated, and the Dutch made Taiwan on Formosa their headquarters, as the Chinese had all along urged them to do.

Of any appreciation of the wider issues of the events in which he was engaged, there is little trace in Bontekoe's account.[1] He had no share in the direct responsibility for them. The conduct of the expedition was entrusted to a Council of seven members, including Reyertsz, who was the President. Bontekoe was not among the number, which included only one of the Captains of ships in the fleet. One member was a Captain of soldiers, and the four remaining members were Merchants. Both the Merchants who successively served on Bontekoe's ship the *Groningen*, Bosschaert and Nieuwenroode, sat on the Council from which the Captain was excluded.

The title of Merchant indicates a rank in the official hierarchy of the Dutch East India Company. The several gradations are: Assistant, Junior Merchant, Merchant, and Senior Merchant. Above that, there are Commanders and Governors, and with them we have reached the sphere of the Governor-General's Council. The two men named were in fact Senior Merchants, and they were considerable personages.

The relations between the Captain of a ship and the Merchant who served on it as a good deal more than a supercargo were difficult. Quarrels were frequent. As Bontekoe indulges in a few palpable hits against Heyn Rol and Cornelis van Nieuwenroode, it is only fair to quote some strictures on the Captain that occur in the latter's reports to the Governor-General and Council. In the *Groningen*, he says, they at one time had as much as five feet of water, " there being, through the carelessness of those who ought to have seen thereto, not a pump that could be used in the whole ship ". " The *Groningen* ", he adds, " is a weak ship, nor is she kept in repair as she ought to be, so that the Lords and Masters will not have service of her so long as would be proper." Having a suggestion to offer for a technical improvement (rattan cords to be used instead of ordinary ropes for anchors), he requests that this may be expressly and strictly ordered, because " otherwise the Captains' pride will scarcely permit them to adopt this ".[1]

No one who has read Bontekoe's journal is likely to take the Merchant's criticisms at their face value. If it reveals anything, it certainly is neither slothfulness nor incompetence. The dogged perseverance and resourcefulness displayed on both the voyage out and the voyage home, that is what after all remains as the strongest impression of Bontekoe's journal.

PLATE II

Behold here Bontekoe, on perilous voyage bent,
By God's good care preserved to all men's wonderment.
Hunger and thirst, storms, fire and sword, he did survive
And stood i' the midst of death, the only man alive.

J.J.D.

[*face p.* 18

Journal or Notable History of the East-Indian Voyages of Willem Ysbrantsz Bontekoe of Hoorn

IN the year of Our Lord 1618, the 28th December, I, William Ysbrantsz Bontekoe of Hoorn, set sail from Texel, being captain of the ship named *New-Hoorn*, manned with 206 men, of size about 1,100 tons, the wind being East.

The 29th day we passed the Heads.

The 30th day, in the evening, we sighted Portland, the wind still Easterly. The 31st day we passed Plymouth.

The 1st January 1619 we passed England's End, the wind being the same, and set our course out to sea, S.W. by S.

The 2nd day the wind veered to S.E.; set our course S.S.W. with a stiff breeze.

The 3rd day the wind changed to South with a stiff breeze; set our course to W.S.W.

The 4th day the wind came S.W. with increasing force, so that we were compelled to take in our top-sails. During the night the wind blew so hard that we took in the foresail and lay to weſtward with one sail.

The 5th at night we shipped three seas, so that the upper deck was half-full of water, and the men began to cry out "We're sinking, we're sinking, the bow gun ports are open!" Hearing that I ran haſtily to the forecaſtle and found the portholes to be closed, whereupon I called out to them "There is no danger!" and said, "Look lively now, let a man go below to see if there may be water in the hold", which was done at once and they found no water in the hold; so I ordered them to bale out the water with leathern buckets. But the men's cheſts were slipping and shifting to and fro by the force of the water, so that they could hardly keep themselves on their feet to bale. So we were forced to break the cheſts to pieces with crowbars; then there was space to bale, and by God's help we got rid of the water. We were then drifting without sails, but the ship swung so mightily that we were compelled to put up the sail again to ſteady her. We lay over to weſtward, the weather being very intemperate, with rain, so that the sea and sky did appear as if welded together, the whole sea foaming as if it were aboil.

The 6th, 7th and 8th day it continued foul weather with rain. We saw that day many sea-fowl, which caused us to believe ourselves near the island Brazil, if such island there be, but we had no sight thereof. That same day we veered and set our head to eastwards, the wind about W.S.W. with tempestuous weather and seeing the storm had long continued and still did not cease, at last through the fearful tossing of the ship and through the stretching of our standing rigging (although we had eased it in two places) our main-mast broke about 5 fathom above the deck. By this break we feared to have lost the mast entirely, therefore we resolved to haul down our top-mast and so if possible keep the main-mast standing, for our journey depended thereon, and if the mast had gone overboard we should have been forced to return to our country; but with great labour and inconvenience we got down the top-mast and let the lower end of it slip through the upper deck, and thus roped the top-mast fast to the main-mast, whereby (to the rejoicing of us all) it then stood firm. This storm continued till the 19th day; we lay now to westward then to southward as the wind shifted.

The 20th day the weather became fair and calm, and while drifting becalmed we bound our mast firmly and drew our main rigging taut and hauled our main topsail out of the top with the top-yard and put that up in place of our main-sail and the top-gallant instead of our main-mast with the top-gallant sail thereon, in which manner we made everything ready to sail and continue our voyage. Set our course for the Canary Islands, S.S.W., the wind being about S.E. with fair weather, and the pleasantness of the weather soon put us at our ease again.

The 21st day saw a sail astern of us that did her best (as we marked) to come near us; we turned to lee and waited for her. When near us we saw it was an East Indiaman that had sailed from Zealand on the 29 Dec. 1618, some days after we sailed from Texel. They were in good order and wanted nothing, nor had they suffered damage by the storm. The ship was named *Nieuw-Zeelandt*, the captain's name was Pieter Tijsz of Amsterdam; we had good company of one another; we sailed near as fast as they though our sails were in a poor way, as related. Our course the same as before.

The 23rd day we again saw a sail on our starboard, and going near found it to be the ship *Enkhuysen* which set sail when we did, also bound for the East Indies. The captain was named Jan Jansz of Enkhuysen. Thus were we three ships in company, and visited one another and related to each other our adventures. Held course for the Canary Islands, which we had sight of and passed; the wind was S.E. with fair weather, we had our topsails up and looked to find the island of St. Anthony for our refreshing, yet by reason of much mist and rain could get no sight of it; therefore, for certainty's sake, set our course for the island of Ile de Mayo or Ile del Foge.[1] Coming there about, it became calm with variable winds and we were forced to tack before we could make it ; we now got parted from our consorts since they came to the Ile de Mayo and we to the Ile del Foge, these islands, lying near together.

Arrived at the island we could find no anchorage, so ran close under the coast into calm water. We had brought with us from Holland a number of small masts and spars which we now got out, pushing them out backwards through the port and hauling them on deck. We sawed a spar of 14 palms through lengthwise and made two fishes and fixed them (besides two other fishes) against the mast, which made our mast as strong as it had been before. At the same time we sent our sloop to the coast to fish and being come close to the shore the Spaniards came with loaded muskets on to the beach and shot at our boat, to show they did not want our men to land ; so they came back to us bringing but little fish. Meanwhile, we were busied with fixing and binding our mast. The mast being ready, we put up our top-mast again and made everything trim and shipshape, at which we all mightily rejoiced, for there our mast stood again so fine it was a pleasure to see. It was near as thick as the pillar of a church. That evening we departed from the lee of the before-mentioned island and set our course to pass the Æquinoctial Line.

While lying by this island there came a great shower of dust off the land, as if there had been a fire, and clung to the rigging of the ship so that it was as white as if strewn with white ashes. The next day, in the morning, when the cook had made ready the breakfast, we saw two sails behind on our lee, took in our topsails and held towards them. Being come near them, they were our two companions, to wit: the ship *Nieuw-Zeelandt* and the ship *Enkhuysen* whom we lost sight of in the night by the islands Ile de Mayo and Ile del Foge; we rejoiced greatly, visited one another on board and related our adventures. They told us how they had been on land on Ile de Mayo for their refreshing, but had found nothing and lost two of their men who were slain by the Spaniards, one of whom came from Hoorn by name Ysbrant Dirckz. The wind was S.E. we kept our course for the Æquinoctial Line. Coming under the line it was calm, but at times we had great gusts of wind with rain, the wind coming from all points so that we wasted three weeks before we could cross the Æquinoctial Line. By night the sea appeared as it were all afire and foaming, it seemed as if sparks of fire shot out from the bow of the ship, but by day it ceased; this (more than common) fire of the sea didgreatly astonish all of us. Set our course to get above the Abrolhos,[1] having a S.E. wind. Coming up to the Abrolhos the wind ſtilled and we feared we could not get to windward of them, yet on nearing them the wind came up, but even so we ran so near that we had sight of the outside islands; thus we came to windward of them by God's help, which rejoiced us all, for had we failed in this we should have been forced to make a long journey with the peril of having many of our men sick. We gave the men that day double ration of food and to every mess a can of Spanish wine. Set our course for the islands of Triſtan d'Acunha. And after we had sailed for several days we were at the height of these same islands yet had no sight of them. The wind now being N.W. we bore eaſtwards to make the Cape of Bonesperance [Good Hope]. After holding this course for some time we saw black-specked gulls of which occasionally we caught some, with ſticks covered with a piece of fat and hooks to them, and so pulled them into the ship by way of paſtime.

The sight of these said gulls is a token of the Cape of Bonesperance being near, for they followed us to the Cape. But there is a truſtworthy sign that the Cape be near or that you be at the height thereof, to wit: When you shall find the compass to hold ſtraight south and North, then look out for land. We did prove this and saw land, namely the Cape of Bonesperance, yet the wind was so ſtrong from the Weſt that we ran with a reefed foresail and durſt not attempt to land. Therefore we called the ship's council together and resolved to sail paſt the Cape, having all our men in good health and no want of water; so we let her go before the wind and continued our way. This was in the laſt of May being five months after we sailed from Holland.

We kept our course along the coaſt to the land of Terra de Natal. In passing this coast the weather was very fair, we visited aboard one another and made good cheer. And the ship *Enkhuysen* being deſtined for the coaſt of Coromandel, she took leave of us and set another course as so to run inside the island of St. Laurentius, otherwise named Madagascar, and so further to the Mayottes to refresh themselves there; we took leave and wished one another a prosperous voyage. We and the ship *Nieuw-Zeelandt* set our course to run outside St. Laurentius, and while we sailed in company we came at times on board of one another and burned the signal light each for a night by turns; but after a time we had some dispute about setting our course and could not agree, yea, it went so far that we separated, each going the course he deemed beſt. *Nieuw-Zeelandt* went 2 degrees further South than we did; they had many sick men at that time.

When we had sailed for a long time after we

separated, being at the height of 23 degrees South of the Æquinoctial Line, we had every day many who fell sick, by reason of which the officers (on the part of the common men) came into the cabin asking that we should go to the island of Madagascar for refreshing; they feared all our men would become sick, for about forty of them lay in their beds and many others did complain of being out of sorts. We therefore resolved with the whole council to hold a ſteady course to the island of Madagascar, to a Bay named Sancta Lucia. Coming near the coaſt we could see no place to bring in the ship; we put out our boat and I went with the boat well-manned to the shore the ship holding in and off near the land. Approaching the coaſt in the boat we found the sea beat so furiously on the shore that there was no chance to get into it; we saw many people come on the shore and one of our men sprang overboard and got to them, but he could not underſtand them, they waved their hands downwards as it were to say that there was a place to land. These folk, as far as we could see, had no fresh food with them; so we must needs go back empty-handed to the ship. And when we came on board (much as we hated it) without refreshments, the sick were grieved beyond measure. We resolved to go out to sea again and hold South to the height of 29 degrees, then veered and sailed Eaſt by South till we came to 17 degrees

South of the Æquinoctial. Then our men again begged that we should make land to seek for refreshment, which we agreed to do seeing that every day more of our men fell sick and some died. Therefore it was resolved to make for the island of Mauritius or the island of Mascarenhas[1] and we set our course between the two, for these islands lie near together. So we struck the East end of the island of Mascarenhas, sailing close round the corner along the shore, found 40 fathom depth close to land and cast anchor, but it was an incommodious place for the ship to lie, being too near the shore. As we lay there the sick crawled out of their berths and would fain have got on land; but the sea running very high, we were afraid to take the sick with us to land; so we sent out the boat to examine the place and coming on land did find the dung of turtles and so returned to the ship; the sick kept on entreating to be put on land for they smelt the air saying: "Were we only on shore we were half cured of our sickness" But the Merchant Heyn Rol would on no account agree thereto; saying that the coast was there too steep, whereby we might easily drift from the land and be cut off from our folk. But the men persisted and almost with clasped hands besought me to bring them on land, so that in the end I let my heart be softened and consented. I went to the Merchant Heyn Rol and asked him if he would agree to it. But he answered, "No, not in any way" Then I said to him, "Then I will take it on myself. I will bring them on land". I went up to the men and said, "Come here, men, help one another into the boat, I will bring you on land". Then the crew helped the sick into the boat, and I ordered a sail to be given them for making a tent, also oil and vinegar, pans to cook with as well as victuals, also cooks to look after the sick and cook for them, then we went directly to the shore.

Being on land they crept together in the grass saying, "We feel better already", and looking about we found a great many doves in the trees, of those blue field-doves. They let themselves be caught by hand or killed with sticks, having no sense to fly away. We took that day about two hundred, brought them to the fire and fell a-boiling and a-roasting for the sick as well as for those in health. We found also many land-turtles; these we boiled with Damascus plums, of which we had brought plenty with us from Holland. I then returned to the ship leaving the sick (about forty in number) with the cooks on shore. Being come on board again we thought it well seeing that the ship lay in a perilous place, that I should go by night with the boat well-manned and sail along the coast to see if we could find a better roadstead to anchor the ship. This I did and sailed the boat close along by the land

and found a good bay of sand to lay up the ship about five miles from the place where she now was. In the bay we went on shore and found there a great lake of water not quite fresh, the reason of which we judged to be that being no more than three ship's lengths from the coast the salt sea water leaked through the sand and so made the other salt as well.

Coming further inland we found great number of geese, doves, grey parrots and other birds, also many land-turtles; seeing as many as twenty to twenty-five lying in the shade of a tree, so that we could have as many as we desired. The geese were not wise enough to fly up when we pursued them, and we beat them to death with sticks without their making a motion to fly. There were also some dodos that had small wings yet could not fly, they were so fat they could scarce move and as they walked dragged their backend along the ground.

And what we most did marvel at, when we held one of the parrots and other birds and squeezed it till it screamed, there came all the others from thereabout as if they would free it and let themselves be caught as well, so we had enough of them to eat. Having seen this we returned with the boat to the ship that (as stated) was about five miles distant from that place. Being again on board we related our adventures, how we had there found a good road in a sand-bay and good and safe anchorage for the ship. At this they all rejoiced exceedingly; we took the boat and brought the news to our men whom we had set ashore in sight of the ship, how we should sail the ship five miles from there and then return to them; with which they were well content.

Whereupon coming on board we weighed and anchored again in the above-mentioned sand-bay in thirty-five fathom and made fast both fore and aft; we let the most of our men land to seek out what they could find; and gave order for eight men to fish with the net in the inland water (which was spoken of) to see if they could get food for the crew. They went to work and caught good fish, that is hard and other fish also, some of the size of salmon and a fine flavour and fat. We found also fresh water: a small river that came down into the sea from the mountains, the which on both sides was grown over with small trees very fair, and the water flowing between as clear as crystal; therefore we brought all our water-barrels to land and filled them from that river leaving them to stand till the time we should go aboard or such time we might think fit.

Here by this water we found also a certain board[1] whereon was written with carved letters that Commander Ariaen Maertsz Block had been there with a fleet of thirteen sail, had there lost several sloops with some of his men, since in landing they had been broken to pieces whereby some men were drowned. In the time of our stay there the sea never ran so strongly.

On this before-mentioned island of Mascarenhas there live no people. Our men wandered over the island almost from end to end and gathered what they would, feeding themselves with the birds and fish. They roasted the birds in good manner on sticks, taking the fat from turtles to smear them with, which made them so delicate it was a pleasure to eat thereof. We found also running water with great eels therein. The men took off their shirts and held them open in the flowing water so catching them in their shirts, and the taste of them was excellent.

Here we saw a thing that amazed all of us; to wit: how the turtles came up out of the sea at morning on the shore and, scratching a hole in the sand, laid their eggs in great numbers, a hundred, nay up to two hundred, scratching sand again over the eggs, which by the sun that did shine by day with great heat, were hatched and young turtles came out from them. We looked at them with wonder for their shells were were no bigger than large nut-shells.

There we found also some sugar palm trees from which we took wine as sweet to the taste as whey.

There we saw goats, but so wild we could not procure

any but one so old that his horns were eaten up with worms. Not fit to be eaten by human beings.

And while we were thus occupied each day, the sick whom we had put on land (as described) did all return to us, all in good health save seven who remained there ; these we afterwards brought back in the boat to the ship.

We tarred the ship within and without, setting open all the scuppers so that air would blow through, and sprinkled her in many places with vinegar ; all to make a good wholesome air in the ship.

We had for our use set up a sundial on land by which we could always see what time of day it was. And as we every day frequently pursued the birds, they at last came to be so fearful of us that they flew away as we approached ; for which reason our chief-mate Jan Piet van Hoorn came on land with a gun to shoot some geese and other birds. And after some shots, the barrel burst out of the stock of the gun so that the screw flew into his head just above the eye by which he lost his eye.

At last we made our ship ready again to set sail. Put up our sails, carried our water aboard and sent a drummer on shore to beat and call all our men together ; we took with us in the boat about a hundred turtles to the ship. We had good store of all things, turtle, birds, fish caught and dried by the men. We in the cabin had a whole barrel of geese laid in vinegar, being part-cooked, in addition also good quantity of fish laid in vinegar to preserve them. And after we had lain there twenty-one days and were got ready, we hoisted sail, crossed over keeping close to the wind, hoping to make the island of Mauritius but came to leeward of it, we had good sight of it but could not come at it. For though we lay so long at the island of Mascarenhas and had our fill of all that was on the island, yet not all our men had recovered their health, there were many who did still complain. For this reason, the officers in name of the men came to us in the cabin to ask were it not advisable to seek another place for our refreshing, because the men were not wholly recovered and we had still to go a long way South before we should come in the monsoon winds that should profit our voyage to Batavia or Bantam, so that it might prove too hard and the men again fall sick. Whereupon after a long deliberation with the ship's council, we thought good to make for the island Sancta Maria that lies close to the coast of Madagascar, before the great Bay of Antongil. Setting our course thereto we had sight of it and sailed round the West end of the island in six, seven or eight fathom of water, seeing the ground through it as clear as day and coming to the inside of the island we found anchor at twelve to thirteen fathom. The people of the country seeing us, set out at once in a proa (being a small boat hewn from a tree) and came aboard us, bringing with them some apples, lemons and rice and fowls ; they gave us to underſtand that they had more of these things on land and brought with them but a vacher. By signs with their mouth they showed us very plainly they had also oxen, sheep, calves, fowls and other creatures ; they shouted moo, ba, cockadoodledo, that was cow, sheep and fowls. We did much marvel at these people. We gave them wine to drink from a silver bowl, yet they had not the sense to know how to drink therefrom, but ſtuck their head or face in the basin and drank as does a beaſt from a bucket, and when the wine was in them they did bawl like as if they were mad.

These people were ſtark naked save for a cloth round their middle to hide their private parts ; they were in colour a yellowish black.

We went every day on land to barter calves, sheep, rice and milk for bells, spoons, brass-handled knives and beads.

The milk they brought within leaves woven together, in form like to a cabbage. From which when we came aboard we cut the leaves, and the milk flowed out. Apples also and lemons we got, but of these they had but few. Therefore, we resolved to sail with the ship two or three mile further, so weighed anchor and came to another place. And coming on land we found there also few apples; but some watermelons and Spanish bacon. We then determined that I should man the boat and go over to the land of Madagascar to see whether there I could traffic for some apples and lemons, which I did. We came to a river and rowed up it a mile or more; and we should have continued further but the trees on both sides of the river did so lean over, yea, till they touched one another, and the waterway in the river became so narrow we were forced to come back. We saw there no people at all, nor fruit, and returned therefore empty-handed. We slept one night on shore and (having been out three days) came in good safety again to the ship. Next day we went again to the island where the ship lay and there procured some more lemons, apples, milk, rice, and bananas.

During the time that we lay there all our men were cured of their sickness and became as cheerful and healthy as when we first sailed out of Holland. Going on shore we took often a musician with us who played on the fiddle, the which did much astonish the people of the country, indeed it was a thing so new to them that they could make nothing of it; they sat and stood around, snapped their fingers, danced and capered and rejoiced right merrily. We found in them no sign of any knowledge of God or any religion, but they had in some places outside their houses the heads of oxen

PLATE III

" They danced and capered and rejoiced right merrily."

[face p. 36

fixed on poles, before which (as it seemed to us) they fell down and worshipped; this appeared mighty strange and without sense of the true God.

The 9th day that we had lain there, our men being as abovesaid, in good health and cheerful, we canted our ship as far as we could venture and cleansed it by scraping and scrubbing, and then set sail, lay to South till at the height of 33 degrees and then veered again eastwards and set our course for the Strait of Sunda. And coming at the height of 5½ degrees, being that of the aforesaid Strait of Sunda,[1] being the 19th day of November, 1619, on that day when drawing the brandy from the cask it was set on fire. For the steward's mate going into the hold (according to custom) in the evening with his small keg to fill it in order to give out each man his measure the following morning, he took with him a candle and stuck the point of it into the wood of a cask which lay a row higher than the one he was to draw from. His keg being filled, he would draw out the candle stick and seeing that he had set it in somewhat firm he pulled it out with an effort. There was a candlewaster on the candle, it fell off and dropped into the bunghole of the cask from which he had just drawn. Thereby the brandy was set afire and flamed up out of the cask, the heads of the cask burst and the burning brandy ran down into the ship where the smith's coals lay.

Presently there was a cry of "Fire! fire!" I was at the time lying on the poop and looked through the railing. Hearing the shouting I went swiftly down to the hold. On coming there I saw no fire and asked "Where is the fire?" They said, "Captain, look there in that cask". I put my arm down the cask and could feel no fire.

The steward's mate by whom the fire was caused came from Hoorn, his name was Keelemeyn. He had two jugs of water with him, and these he had thrown on it, so that the fire seemed to be quenched. But I called for water from the deck which was brought straightway with leathern buckets and we poured till we saw no more sign of fire. We went out of the hold but in the space of half-an-hour they began again to call "Fire! fire!" at which we were all very much alarmed. On coming into the hold we saw that the fire was blazing upwards from below, for the casks stood three and four high and the fire had burned through the brandy into the smith's coal; we went to work again with leathern buckets and threw so much water it was a marvel. Now again came a new trouble, for our throwing of water into the smith's coals made such a stinking sulphurous smoke that we were like to be choked with faintness. I stayed most of the time in the hold to keep order, and caused from time to time other men to come in the hold to refresh them.

I am afraid that already then many never got out of the hold and were stifled to death, not being able to find the hatches. I myself was many times quite confused in seeking and laid my head on the casks to get breath, turning my face to the hatch; at last I ran out and going to the Merchant Heyn Rol said: "Mate, it will be best to throw the gunpowder overboard" But the Merchant Heyn Rol could not consent to this, he answered: "If we throw the powder overboard we may put out the fire and coming afterwards in fight with our enemy, should we be taken (having no gunpowder), how should we answer for this?"

The fire would not be put out, and no man could remain longer in the hold for the stinking smoke (as described). We then hewed holes in the orlop deck and threw into them mightily with water, as well as through the hatches; yet it was in vain. Our longboat we had put out three weeks before this and towed it behind us, and the yawl, too, that stood on the poop had been put out because it stood in the way and prevented the men forming a line with water buckets; and as there was great dismay in the ship, which may be understood (for the fire and the water was before our eyes, and no help to be expected from anyone on earth, for we were alone, no land, ship or ships to be seen), therefore many of the crew went overboard and crept by stealth with their heads under the chainwales that they should not be seen, then let themselves fall into the water and swam to the yawl and longboat, they then climbed in and hid themselves under the thwarts and decks till they thought they had men enough.

Heyn Rol, the Merchant, came by chance on to the stern walk and marvelled to see so many men in the boat and yawl. They called to Heyn Rol and said they meant to row off and if he would go with them he must let himself down by the man-rope and so come to them in the boat. Heyn Rol let himself be persuaded and climbing down the man-rope came to them in the boat. Heyn Rol said: "Men, let us wait till the Captain comes", but he had no command over them, for as soon as they had Heyn Rol with them they cut the hawsers, and rowed straightway from the ship. And as I was busy with the men making shift to put out the fire wherever possible, there came other men running to me, crying out in great alarm: "O! dear Captain, what must we do? The sloop and boat are gone from the ship, they are rowing off!" I said to them: "Are the boat and yawl gone? So! They have gone on such terms they shall not come back". Thereupon I ran hastily on deck and saw them rowing away. The sails of the ship at the time were lying against the mast, the mainsail was brailed up. I called to the men hastily: "Haul the sails round! Let us see if we can overtake them and run them down. The devil take them!" We set the sails to the wind and went after them. On coming up with them, at about three ship's length athwart us they rowed across for they did not want to come to us but rowed against the wind away from the ship. Then I said: "Men, we have (next to God) no help but ourselves, as you see. Let each one set to work (as well as he can) to put out the fire, go straightway to the powder store and throw the powder overboard so that the fire does not lay hold of the powder". And this was done. Then I with all the carpenters went overboard with hollow chisels and augers to bore holes in the ship, our purpose being to let a fathom or so of water into the ship so as to smother the fire from below; but we could not get through the ship because there was so much ironwork in the way. In short, the terror was that in the ship is beyond my power to express: the groans and screams were fearful beyond measure. Now again we courageously fell to throwing of water, by which the fire did seem to abate, but a short time after the fire came into the oil; then our courage was lost entirely, for the more water we threw, the worse the fire seemed to become, so high did it flame up through the oil. Then there arose such crying, groaning and shrieking in the ship as caused a man's hair to rise on his head, yea, the vehemence of fear and terror was so great that cold sweat poured from men's faces; yet we did continue to pour on water and throw powder overboard until the end when the fire laid hold of the powder. About sixty half casks of powder we had thrown overboard, yet had in the ship still about three hundred with which we blew up every man of us. The ship burst into a hundred thousand pieces; 119 persons were in the ship when it was blown up.

I stood then when it came to pass, near the main gangway up on deck and about sixty persons who were handing the waterbuckets stood right in front of the main mast; these were all carried off together and shivered to bits till you could not see where the pieces were of one man or another. And I, Willem Ysbrantsz Bontekoe, at that time captain, was blown up with them into the air; I know no better than that I should die there with them. I raised my hands and arms to Heaven and cried: "There I go, O Lord! be merciful to me, poor sinner!" I believed this to be my death, yet in being blown up I retained my understanding, and did feel a lightness in my heart that seemed to be mingled with a certain cheerfulness and I came down again into the water among the boards and fragments of the ship that was all to pieces. Lying in the water I received such new courage as if I had been a new man. And looking round I perceived the mainmast to lie

PLATE IV

The Shipwreck.

[face p. 42

on my one side and the foremast on the other. I climbed into the mainmast and laid myself down thereon and took a view of what was done and said: "O God, see how this beautiful ship is destroyed, like Sodom and Gomorrah".

Lying thus I saw no living creature whatsoever way I looked, and while I lay in thought, there a young man did bubble up beside me, beating with hands and feet and he got hold of the point of the prow (that had drifted up again) saying: "I am all right". Then I looked round and said: "O God, is there still a man alive?" This young man was named Harmen van Kniphuysen, from the Eider region.[1] I saw near him a spar or yard floating and because the mainmast (on which I lay) rolled continually from side to side so that I could not well remain on it, I said to him: "Push that spar towards me, I will lie on it, then pull me to you and we can sit together". This he did and I came to him. The reason why I could not otherwise have come to him was that in being blown up I was sorely hit. My back was much hurt, I had two holes in my head, nay, it was so bad that I thought, "O Lord! in a little while I shall be dead". Yea, it seemed that my sight and hearing were going. We sat here side by side each with his arm round a rib of the ship's forepart. We stood up and looked out for the longboat and yawl; and at last had sight of them but they were so far off that we could hardly see if it were the head or the stern that faced us. The sun was come down to the water ready to set. I said to my comrade: "Harmen, it seems that our hope is lost, for it is late, the sun goes down, the boat and sloop are so far we can scarce see them; the ship is gone to pieces and we cannot endure long on the wreck; therefore let us pray God Almighty to deliver us". We did so and prayed God earnestly for deliverance; which was sent us, for as we again raised our eyes, there were the sloop with the boat nigh us at which we rejoiced exceedingly. And straightway I called out: "Save the Captain! save the Captain!" Hearing which they were glad and cried: "The Captain is still alive! the Captain is still alive!" and then rowed near to the wreck and lay there both yawl and boat; they dared not come close for they feared a piece of the wreck might cut through the yawl or boat. The young man Harmen van Kniphuysen had still enough spirit to jump from the wreck and swim to the boat. He had not suffered much injury from the blowing up, but I called out: "If you want me you must fetch me, for I am so hurt that I cannot swim". Then the trumpeter sprang out of the boat with a sounding line (which they still had) and brought me the end. I made it fast round my middle and they pulled me to the boat, and so I came (the Lord be praised!) into the boat. Being in the boat I came aft beside Heyn Rol, Willem van Galen and the second-mate, named Meyndert Krijnsz, of Hoorn, who marvelled greatly that I was still alive. I had caused a little deckhouse to be made in the stern of the boat—right across it—that might hold two men; I crept therein and thought I must take counsel with myself, for I surmised I had not long to live through the blow on my back and the two holes in my head; but nevertheless I said to Heyn Rol and the others: "Stay this night by the wreck, to-morrow when it is day we shall salve some victuals, and mayhap find a compass to help us find land". For in the yawl and boat there was neither compass or chart or sextant, nor scarce any food or drink; with such haste had they left the ship. In fact, they said that the chief mate, Jan Piet, of Hoorn, had taken the compass from the binnacle; it seemed he feared already that they might leave the ship, which they did in spite of his precaution.

Now while I lay in that hole or deckhouse, the Merchant told the men to put out the oars and set them to rowing, for all the world as if he thought to have land when it was day. But when day was come we had lost the wreck no less thoroughly then the land. They were sore dismayed, and came to look in the hole where I lay whether I were alive or not, and seeing me still alive they spoke; "Oh, dear, Captain! What shall we do ? We have lost the wreck and see no land, we have neither food or drink, nor sextant nor chart nor compass ! What counsel do you give ? " Thereupon I said : " Men, I ought to have been hearkened to when I said last night that you should stay by the wreck at night, so that we might get victuals, for the meat and bacon and cheese floated about my legs that I could scarce move through them ". They said : " Dear Captain, come out to us ". I said : " I am so lame that I can hardly move ; if you want me to come out you must help me " They then came and helped me out and I sat down, looked over the men and they were rowing. I asked forthwith : " Men, how much food is there in the boat ? " And they brought about seven or eight pounds of bread for the whole company ; we had two empty barrels and we laid the bread therein. I said further : " Men, pull in your oars, you must do otherwise, for you will be spent with fatigue and we have no food to give. Pull in your oars ". Then they said : " What must we do then ? " But I said : " Take off your shirts and make sails thereof ". They said : " We have no sail-thread ". I said : " Take the buffer-pads from the boat and pluck them loose and twist them into sail thread, from the rest make matting for sheet and gaff ". Thereupon every man of them took off his shirt, and they tacked them together for sails, and those in the yawl did the same. I then counted our men and found in the longboat forty-six and in the yawl twenty-six persons, thus together seventy-two.

There was a blue reefer coat and a cushion in the boat; these were given to me. The reefer I put on and placed the cushion on my head, for (as I related) I had two holes in my head. The barber we had with us in the boat, but he had no medicaments; so he chewed some bread and laid it therewith on the wounds, by which (with God's favour) I was cured; I also offered to take off my shirt but they would not allow of this; they had care for me to keep me alive. We let ourselves drift the whole day, being busied meanwhile to make the sails. By evening they were ready, we set them up and began to sail. This was the 20th day of November, 1619. We then began to set our course by the stars, for we knew well enough where the stars should rise and set; so we set our course in the night time.

By night the cold was so great that the men's teeth chattered, yet by day so hot that one felt like dying of heat, for the sun was mostly right overhead. The 21st, 22nd and 23rd November we put together a sextant to take our height; cast a quadrant on the quarter deck and drew a stick with a cross piece therefrom. We had the coffin-maker, Teunis Sybrantsz, of Hoorn, in the boat, he had a pair of compasses. He also had some knowledge of drawing a stick so that together in that way we made and shaped a sextant, with which we shot the sun. I also cut a sea-chart on the board aft and laid the island of Sumatra therein, with the island of Java and the Strait of Sunda that runs in between the two islands. And that same day wherein we lost the ship, in the afternoon I had taken the height of the sun and found 5½ degrees South of the Æquinoctial Line, and the specification on the chart showed about ninety miles from land. I also cut a compass therein, and measured each day with a pair of compasses by guesswork and set the course seventy miles to the side or above the hole, so as the better to know what direction we must take if we saw land. We sailed thus by the shooting with our sextant and by our measuring.

From the seven or eight pounds of bread I gave each man every day his portion so long as it might last, but it was soon finished. Each man had every day a piece the size of a finger-joint. We had no drink; therefore when it rained we took down our sails and spread them across the boat and caught up the water on the sail and stored it in our two barrels, and when these were filled we put them aside for a day when it was dry and no rain fell. I cut off the toe of a shoe and each man came to the barrel and filled it and drank and returned to the place where he had sat. And although we were in such distress, the men said : " Captain, take as much as you will, for in any case it is not enough for all of us." Seeing their courtesy, I would not have more than they did. Sailing in this manner with yawl and boat and because the boat sailed faster than yawl and seeing there was no man in the yawl who had knowledge of navigation, therefore those who were in the yawl (when they came near to us) entreated that they might come over into the boat and said : " Dear Captain, take us over so that we may be together ". They feared they might drift away from us. But the men in the boat were against this and said : " Captain, should we take them over, we'd all be done for, for the boat cannot carry all the men ". So they were forced to keep off the boat.

The distress among us was great ; we had no more bread and could see no land. I continually made the men believe that we were near land, so they should keep of good courage, but they began to murmur against it among themselves and said one to another : " The Captain may say we are sailing towards land, but maybe we are sailing away from land ".

On a certain day (when it seemed that we could endure no longer without food) God Almighty sent sea-gulls to fly over the boat, verily as if they desired to be caught, for they flew almost into our hands, letting themselves be caught. We plucked off their feathers and cut them into small pieces and gave some to each man, we ate them raw and it tasted to me as good as any food that ever I did eat in my life; yea, it tasted as sweet honey in my mouth and throat. Had there only been more of it, it was just enough or hardly so much as to keep us alive, and no more.

And seeing that no land yet came in sight we became so disheartened that the men resolved (when those on the yawl again begged they might come to us) to take them in, for as there came no deliverance by land we feared that we must die of hunger and thirst, and if we must die then we resolved rather to die all of us together. We then took over the men from the yawl into the boat and took all the oars out of the yawl with the sails, and placed them in the boat. We had then in the boat a sprit-sail, foresail, mainsail and mizzen-sail. We had also about thirty oars, we laid them across the thwarts as an orlop. The boat was so deep that the men could sit comfortably on their bottoms under the oars, so we set one-half of the men beneath the oars and the other half above the oars and could thus dispose the men conveniently. We were then seventy-two persons in the boat; and looked upon one another most woefully, having neither food or drink. There was now no more bread, nor did the sea-gulls come any more and it would rain no more.

Now when there seemed again the poorest prospect

PLATE V

" Seeing no land yet came in sight, we . . resolved to take them in."

of keeping our lives, all unforeseen there came (by the Lord's mercy) bursting up out of the sea a school of flying fishes about the size of a large smelt, like a flock of sparrows they flew into the boat. Then there was a general grabbing and snatching, each doing his utmost to catch them. We divided them among us and ate them raw, they tasted sweet as honey, but they did not carry us very far. It refreshed us more or less and prevented (by God's help) that any of us died, which was a marvel, for the men were already beginning to drink sea-water in spite of my warnings. I said to them : "Men, drink no salt water for it will not cure your thirst ; you will get dysentry therefrom and die". Others chewed shot and musket-balls, others drank their own urine. I drank my own urine as long as it was good, but it became later unsuitable for drinking.

Our distress became every day greater and heavier to bear, and the men began to look with such despair, distrust and malevolence at one another as if almost they would devour each other, verily they did speak of it among themselves, deeming fit to eat first the boys, and when these were finished, they should draw lots who should be the next one ; I was sore troubled at this and in great distress of mind prayed to God Almighty that in his Fatherly compassion he would have mercy and not let it come to this ; that he would not afflict us beyond our endurance, knowing the weakness of his creatures. I cannot express how the fear of this proposal did oppress me, the more because (so I judged) I saw some who would have begun to kill the boys, yet (with God's help) I dissuaded them, praying for the boys and said: "Men, let us not do this thing. God will deliver us, for we cannot be far from land, as shown by our daily measurements and shooting". They answered: "You have told us that many times, yet we find no land; yea, maybe we are sailing away from the land"; they being much dissatisfied. Whereat they fixed with me the time of three days, after which if we came not in sight of land, the boys should be eaten. Truly a desperate resolve! So I prayed to God most fervently to look graciously upon us and bring us before that time to land, that we might commit no abominations before His eyes. The time passed and our distress was so great that we could bear it no longer. We thought many times: were we but on land, it would not matter if we might eat nothing but grass. I diverted the men with such comfortable counsel as I could at that time call to mind. I said they must be of good courage, that the Lord would provide, but I myself was but fainthearted, would give comfort to others yet was myself in need to be comforted. I spoke many words that my heart misgave me. We endured and suffered thus together and became so faint and feeble that we had scarce strength to stand. Heyn Rol, the Merchant, had come to such a pass that where he sat there he stuck and could come no further. I had so much energy left that I could move from one end of the boat to the other. We drifted thus as God directed till the second day of December, 1619, being the thirteenth day of our losing the ship. It was then a clouded sky with rain and calm; we loosened the sails, spread them across the boat and crept all together under the sails and filled our barrels full of water. The men had very little clothing by their setting out with such haste and their shirts were made into sails, as before related; most of the men had no more on than a linen drawers and the upper part of them bare. They crept in this way together under the sails (to get warmth) and I stood at the time at the rudder and did surmise we were nearing land. I hoped it would clear while I stood at the helm, but it continued misty. I became so cold through the fog and damp in the air that I could keep no hold on the rudder any longer therefore called to one of the quartermasters and said: "Come and relieve me of the helm, for I can hold out no longer". Then came the quartermaster and relieved me and I crept under to the men to gain warmth.

The quartermaster had not stood an hour at the helm when the mist began to clear and he looked and forthwith he saw land. He cried out with great rejoicing: "Come out men, there is land, just in front of us! Land! Oh, Land!" You should have seen with what speed we came out from under the sail. We set up the sails again and sailed to the land; we came that same day to land. God Almighty be praised, who thus answered our prayers and entreaties; for we prayed morning and evening with fervent worship of God and sang a psalm before and after our prayer, for we had a few psalmbooks with us. Most of the time I had acted as clerk, but later when the reader came out of the yawl into our boat he did it himself.

On coming to the land, the sea ran so high on to the shore that we dared not land, but we found on the inside of the island (for island it was[1]) an inlet; there we let fall the grapnel and having another one we set it on to the land so that the boat was moored head and stern, and we sprang (as well as we were able) all men on shore, going each his way to forage. But as soon as I was on land I fell on my knees, kissing the earth with joy and thanking God for His mercy and compassion that He had not tried us but thus far helped us out; for this day was the last of those after which the men had resolved to attack the boys and eat them. By this was shown that the Lord was the best Steersman Who did guide and steer us till we made the land, as I have related.

We found on this island abundance of coco-nuts,

but could not find (what we sought) fresh water ; we satisfied ourselves therefore with the sap of the young coco-nuts which was a good drink. And we ate of the old nuts that had become hard ; this we did too eagerly, without forethought, for the same night we all fell grievously sick with such distressful pain and cramps in the stomach and belly that we were like to burst. We crept together in the sand, each one groaning his hardest ; after that purging of the bowels did begin to work, by which we felt immediate relief ; the next day we were recovered and almost made the round of the island. We found there no people, but did see signs of people having been there. Here was no other thing to eat save coco-nuts. Our men told me they had sight of a snake that was as much as a fathom thick, but I saw it not myself.

This island lies about fourteen to fifteen miles from the coast of Sumatra. We brought as many coco-nuts as we could into the boat for provision, the old nuts to eat and the young ones to drink from. At evening we weighed and went off from the island to the coast of Sumatra ; the following day we had sight of it. We came near, kept in along the shore with the wind behind us, held East until the nuts were finished. Then the men desired again to go on land ; we sailed close along the breakers on the coast, but found no place to land because the sea ran so high.

Then we resolved that four or five men should spring overboard and see if they could swim through the surf to land and walk along the shore and see if they could not see any opening to come in with the boat. Which was done. They sprang overboard, pushed through the breakers to land and walked along the shore, and we sailed with the boat near the coast.

At last they found a river. And they took off their hose and waved to us that we should come in there. Seeing which we sailed directly thereto. Being come, there lay a bank right before the mouth of the river on which the seas beat with such force that I said; "Men, I shall not go in here, save with the consent of every man, for should the boat capsize you shall not reproach me with it". And being asked, every man in his turn, what they said, they answered, Yea, they would venture it. Then I said: "I venture my life with yours". I hastily gave order that at the stern of the boat they should put out an oar on each side and two men at each oar. I stood at the helm to keep the boat straight ahead. In this way we went into the breakers. The first sea that came plunged the boat half full of water. I called out: "Bale out, men! Bale out!" And they baled, with hats and shoes and with the empty barrels we had in the boat; and threw most of the water out. Then came the next sea; this threw the boat full of water almost up to the thwarts, whereby she lay so vilely as if ready to sink. And I called to them : "Men, hold straight, hold straight! Bale out, bale out, or we are all dead men". We drove straight before the sea and baled out all the water we could. Then came the third sea and that fell short of us so that we took in but little water and then it was at once calm water. So with God's help we came through. We tasted the water and it was already fresh, at which we all rejoiced exceedingly, and we moored the boat to the land on the right-hand side of the river. Coming on to the land it was overgrown with long grass and looking round we saw beans among the grass like to the Eider beans. Then all men sought for them and ate them. I myself did my best, thinking : "I had better try to get my share", and our men walked a little beyond. There they found a fire with some tobacco lying beside it, at which we rejoiced greatly. It seemed that people of the country had been there, kindled fire and having smoked tobacco had left some of it lying either by accident or on purpose. We had two axes in the boat ; with these we hacked down trees and cut off the branches, and made fires in five or six places. There our men in companies of ten or twelve stood or sat around and smoked tobacco. When it was evening we made blazing fires and set a watch in three places for fear of the inhabitants of the country, for there was no moon.

Now that same night we became so ill from the beans which we had eaten that we were like to burst with the pain and cramps in our bellies (the same as overtook us before with the coco-nuts). And while we were lamenting, the inhabitants of the land came with intent to slay us all, as I shall hereafter describe. The watch we had set became aware of them just in time and came to us and said : " Men, what shall we do ? Here they come ! " We had no arms but two axes and one rusty sword, and, moreover, we were ill (as related) from the beans. We resolved however, not to let ourselves be slain so easily, and taking up burning faggots in our hands, we set off towards them in the dark ; the sparks of fire flew out over the ground which in the darkness was terrible to behold. Besides they knew not if we were armed or not. They took flight away from us, behind the woods, and we returned again to our fires, and remained so the whole night in fear and alarm sitting and standing by the fire, but I and the Merchant Heyn Rol went into the boat, not trusting ourselves on the land.

In the morning when it was day and the sun had risen, there came three of the inhabitants out of the woods on to the beach. We sent to them three of our men who could speak some Malay for they had been in the East Indies before and partly learned the speech. And being come to them the three inhabitants asked them what people we were, and they said: "We are Hollanders who by misfortune of fire have lost our ship and are come here to trade for refreshments if you have such". They answered they had fowls and rice, which we greatly desired. Then they came to us near the boat and asked if we also had arms. We gave answer: "Yea, plenty of arms, muskets, powder and shot". I had the sails put over the boat so that they could not see what was within. Then they brought us rice, that was boiled, and several fowls. We inquired of one another what money we had and put it together. One brought out five, another six, another twelve, some more, some less, reales of eight, so that altogether we had about eighty reales of eight, from which money we paid for the fowls and rice they brought us. Having these I said to the men: "Now men, sit down together and let us first eat our bellyful and then see how it is". The which we did. The meal being finished we consulted what was to be done in order to supply ourselves with what was needful. And as we were not sure of our latitude, we inquired of them the name of their country, but could not understand it clearly, but thought it to be Sumatra. They waved their hands downwards that Java lay there and named Jan Coen, that he was our Chief there in Java; which was true, for Jan Pieterszoon Coen, of Hoorn, was at that time General[1], so that we then partly knew our bearings and conjectured that we were to the windward of Java; for we had no compass and had always been in doubt if our measurements were secure; we were thereby greatly assured of our reckoning.

But as we needed more victuals to continue our voyage, we resolved that I with four of the men in a proa should go up the river to the village that lay a way up, and with the money we had, buy victuals there as much as we could procure. Which I did and we went up the river.

Being come into the village we bought rice and fowls, which we sent to the boat to Heyn Rol the Merchant, giving order that each should have his portion so there should be no quarrelling, and I with the four men in the village then had two or three fowls boiled with some rice; we sat down together and ate as much as we would. There was drink too, which they take out of the trees, it is so strong that a man may well become drunk by it. We drank thereof with each other, after we had eaten. While we ate, the people of the town sat round about us and looked upon every bite we took.

After our meal I bought a buffalo for 5½ pieces of eight, but the buffalo being paid for we could not get hold of him because of his great wildness; did thereby lose much time, and it growing late in the day, I would return to the boat with the four men: the buffalo, so I

PLATE VI

" There stood a great company of the inhabitants chattering most vehemently amongst themselves."

[face p. 60

thought, we could catch the following day. But hereover the four men did beg me to allow they might ſtay there that night, saying that at night when the beaſt lay down they would secure him. Although I did advise againſt this, at laſt by their continued insiſtence I yielded. I took leave of them and we wished one another good-night.

Coming to the side of the river where the proa lay, there ſtood a great company of the inhabitants chattering moſt vehemently amongſt themselves. It looked as if some would have that I should go, others not. I seized one or two from their number by the arm and pushed them to the proa to row, juſt as if I ſtill was maſter, whereas I was but half servant. They looked moſt frightful bullies, yet let themselves be commanded and two went with me into the proa. The one sat fore, the other aft, each with a paddle in the hand and pushed off. They had each a kriss ſtuck in their side, being a weapon like a poniard with a grained blade.

When we had gone some diſtance, the one from behind came to me, for I sat in the middle of the prow, and signed he would have money. I felt in my inner pocket and took out a "kwartje" and gave it to him. He ſtood and looked at it, not knowing what to do; then he took it and folded it into the cloth he had round his middle. The front man seeing his fellow had received something, came also to me and showed that he too would have something. Seeing which I again took a "kwartje" from my pocket and gave it to him. He stood and looked at it also; it seemed as if he were in doubt to take the money or to attack me, which they could easily have done for I was unarmed and they had (as described) each a kriss in his belt.

There I sat like a sheep between two wolves, in a thousand fears, God knows what I felt. We were going with the stream (for there was a strong current). About half-way (to the boat) they fell to jabbering and shouting, by all signs it seemed that they meant to make an end of me. Perceiving this I was so fearful that my heart quaked and trembled with fear; therefore I turned to God and prayed for mercy, and that He would give me understanding what were best for me to do in this situation. And it seemed that a voice within me said I should sing, which I did although I was in such distress; and I sang so that the trees and woods were filled with the sound, for the river on both sides was grown with high trees. And when they saw and heard that I thus began to sing they began to laugh and gaped till you could see down their throats, and it appeared they thought I did not fear them, yet in my heart it was far otherwise than I trust they thought.

In this wise I proved indeed that a man can sing even

from fear and anxiety, and herewith we came so far that I saw the boat where it lay. Then I ſtood up and waved to our men (who ſtood by the boat). On being aware of men, they came haſtily along the river bank and I signed to the two who had brought me they should bring the proa to land, which they did, and I signed they should go before me, for I thought, " So doing at leaſt you shall not ſtab me from behind ". Thus I came again to our company.

Having (by God's grace) escaped these perils and terrors, when we were come to the boat, the two inhabitants asked where our men slept. We answered : " Under those tents ", for our men had made tents of branches into which they crept. They asked also where I and Heyn Rol, the merchant slept ; we said : "In the boat under the sail". They then returned to the village. I thereupon related to Heyn Rol and the other men how I had fared and that I had bought a buffalo in the town which we could not lay hold of that evening ; and the four men whom I had taken with me had begged they might abide there the night so they could take the beaſt when he lay down and bring him aboard, to which after their long insiſtence I gave consent, with the underſtanding they should return to us with the beaſt, early to-morrow morning.

Having related this and more of our happenings, we all lay down to sleep for the night. In the morning when it was day, yes, even when the sun had risen a good way, we had no sight of either man or beast. Thereupon we fell in doubt that all might not be well with our four comrades, and after some more time of waiting we saw two of the inhabitants coming towards us driving a beast before them. When they were come to us, and I saw the beast, I said it was not the same that I had bought and paid for. Our steward could understand them in part, he asked them why they had not brought the same beast which I bought and also where our men were (that is the four who men went with me to the village). They answered that they could not lay hold of that beast and that our men were coming with another; by this we were partly satisfied. And because this beast which was brought by the two blacks was so unruly and sprang wildly, I said to Willem van Galen, the sergeant: "Take the axe in your hand and hamstring the beast so that he does not escape us; for we can suffer no loss". The which he did; he took the axe and hamstrung it so that it fell to the ground.

Then these two blacks set up a marvellous crying and screaming, at which there came running from out of the woods two or three hundred men (or thereabouts with intent to cut us off from the boat and slay us all together; but we were warned in time by three of our company who had been lighting a fire a space beyond

PLATE VII

" There came running from out of the woods two or three hundred men."

[face p. 64

us; for they came running to us and said: "They are coming!"

I stepped a little out of the trees and saw there some forty of them come out of the wood, and I said to our men: "Stand fast, we need not fear these people, we have men enough". But there came so many of them and continually more, till it seemed there was no end to it, they all had shields and swords and appeared like monsters, whereby I was dismayed and began to call out: "Men, each to the boat as quick as you can, for if they cut us off from the boat we are dead men!"

So we started a-running, all of us to the boat, those who could not get near the boat took to the river and swam. They followed us to the boat and when we came into the boat, it was all unready for us to go aboard thus in haste and put away from the shore; for the sails were laid across the boat for a tent. They were at our heels when we scrambled into her, and struck our men with assegais in their bodies (as they climbed over) so that their bowels fell out. With our two axes we defended ourselves the best we could and our rusty sword did great deeds, for in the stern of the boat stood a huge fellow (who was a baker) and hewed lustily therewith.

We had a grapnel at the stern and another to seaward at the bow. I having climbed in about where the mast is, called out to the baker: "Cut the rope, cut the grapnel rope off", and he cut, he cut, but it would not break. Seeing which I went aft, took the rope and laid it flat on the stern and I said "Now cut it", and he cut it off at once. Then our men at the head of the boat near the grapnel rope pulled the boat out to sea. The blacks came after us into the water, but the coast here being very steep they were soon off the ground and had to leave us; we fished up our men who had swum in the river and hauled them into the boat. Hardly were the men in the boat when God Almighty caused wind to come suddenly from the land, which up to that time had blown from the sea. Verily a marvellous sign of God's merciful hand. We hoisted our sails and sailed straight out of the inlet in one tack against the high breakers and this time got over the bank (on which we had been in such peril on coming in, as related) so that but little water came into the boat.

The blacks or inhabitants of the country did not think we should be able to come out and they ran on to the point of land with intent to take us there and kill us; but it seemed that such was not the will of God, for the boat rode high and straight and sprang up against the sea; in this way by God's help we got out of the inlet. When we were outside, the baker (who had fought so well with the sword) became all blue in the face, for he had been wounded in the belly right above his navel and the weapon was poisoned, by which the wound was blue all round it; this I cut out to prevent that the poison should spread, but it was in vain, he died before our eyes. Being dead we put him overboard and let him float. Then we took count of our men and found that we had lost sixteen of our company, to wit, eleven they had slain on shore, and the baker we had laid overboard, and the other four men who had stayed in the town. At this we all together were sorely grieved and did lament then, but nevertheless thanked the Lord that we were not all slain in that place.

For my own part I judged that next to God, those four men who stayed in the town had saved my life, for if they had come with me to the boat when I went away, so they (to wit the blacks) would have slain all five of us, so I verily believe; for when I stood on the side of the river with that big crowd they disputed together (as related) as to my going away, but I made signs to shew that the following day I should come to them with all my men. Then it appeared they thought: "Let us make no trouble, we shall then be able to cut them down and kill them with little trouble" They believed that I should not abandon my four men, and looked upon them as sufficient surety; yet they were out in their reckoning. However, it was a pitiful business that we were forced to leave our men there, but I surmise that they had already slain them.

We set our course and sailed before the wind along the coaſt. We had ſtill eight fowls and a small ſtore of rice in the boat, and that for fifty-six persons which we then were. Verily, but a small portion for so many men! We divided it and gave each his share. These victuals spent, we consulted together that it were beſt to seek land again, seeing we had already great hunger and in the sea we could get nothing at that time to feed on. We therefore turned again towards land, and seeing a bay we sailed into it. We saw on the shore before us many people ſtanding together, and went towards them, but they did not wait for us but ran away. We found there no victuals, but there was fresh water, of which we drank as much as we would; filled up our two barrels with it, and took the boat round the cliffs. There we found small oyſters and winkles; and each one gathered his pocketful. At the place where we loſt our four men, I had bought a hatful of pepper, which was now a good seasoning to the oyſters and warmed our ſtomachs mightily.

We sailed again out of the bay and ſtood out to sea to continue our voyage. Being ſtill not far from the land we fell into a ſtorm of wind so that we were forced to take down our sails, these we furled across the boat and crept everyman under sails and let ourselves drift at God's mercy till some two hours before day, then the wind lessened and we had again fair weather. We then came up and hoisted our sails again. We then met a headwind and tacked away from the shore. It seemed that God would preserve us from greater danger, for had we not encountered this storm and contrary wind we should have held along the coast and likely enough run into the watering-place which lay near to, in Sumatra, where our nation was used to land; and here they were now bitter enemies to the Hollanders for shortly before this time many Hollanders had been slain on going in for water. Now when day was come we saw three islands lying ahead of us[1]; we resolved to sail thither, thinking there were no people thereon, but we had hope to find something to refresh ourselves; we came there that same day. There we found at once fresh water and saw great reeds growing as thick as a man's leg, these we cut down with our axes. These reeds are named bamboos We pierced through the joints with a stick all save the lowest joint, we poured water into these and put stoppers on and by these means we got as much as two tons of fresh water into the boat. We found also palm trees which in their tops were so tender as it were the pith of rushes; these we also cut down and took with us such as were good for victuals. Our men wandered through all the island foraging, yet could find nought else of any worth.

I went apart from the men and seeing a hill (the

highest in the island) I went up and looked all round, being sore oppressed and troubled in spirit because (so I deemed) it lay most on me to find a way, and seeing that I had never been in the East Indies and had no steersman's instruments, in chief no compass (as related) I judged it best in my extremity to trust myself to the Lord, for I was truly at my wits end, even as many times before. Therefore I fell on my knees and prayed to God, beseeching Him that since He had hitherto saved and preserved me under His merciful wings and rescued me from fire and water, hunger and thirst and the power of evil men, in His Fatherly goodness He would vouchsafe to preserve me further and open the eyes of my understanding to find the right way whereby we should be restored to our Nation and Friends. Yea! with deep sighs I prayed: " O Lord, shew us the way and guide me; yet if Thy wisdom deem it best not to bring me in safety to our Nation, suffer then (if it be Thy divine will) some of our company to be saved so that people may know how things have gone with us and our ship ". And having this spoken with God, I stood up to go down again, and as before once and again cast my eyes round about me, and behold I saw on my right hand that the clouds dispersed from the land by which the horizon became clear; then I saw two high blue mountain tops, and immediately it came into my mind that at Hoorn I did hear Willem

PLATE VIII

"Therefore I fell on my knees and prayed to God."

[face p. 70

Cornelisz Schouten[1] (who had been two or three times in the East Indies) say that at the corner of Java were two high blue mountains; and we had come along the coast of Sumatra that lay on the left hand while these I saw to the right hand; and in between was a gap where I saw no land, and I knew that the strait of Sundra ran in between Java and Sumatra, therefore I was surely convinced that we were in the right way and so went cheerfully down from the hill to the merchant and told him I had seen two such mountains. When I had told him this the clouds were again spread over them so that they could not be seen. I told him also what I had heard Willem Cornelisz Schouten tell, and what I concluded therefrom, to wit: That I did verily believe that we were right before the strait of Sunda. Then said the merchant: "Well, Captain, if such is your mind of it, let us then call the men together and sail thereto, for your conjecture and reasoning are in my opinion well founded".

Thereupon we called the men together and they brought water in the bamboos and the tops of palm trees which we had gathered for victuals into the boat, and we put off; we had the wind with us and set our course straight for the gap, and at night by the stars. About midnight we saw a fire which we took at first for a ship; and thought it to be a carack[2]; but on coming near found it was a small island which lies in the strait of Sunda named Dwars-in-de-weg[1], and we passed that island. Some little time after we saw another fire on the other side, to wit starboard; we passed that also, I thought them to be good signs of fishers. In the morning at break of day it was calm; we were then on the inside of the island of Java[2]. We sent a man to climb the mast; he looked ahead and called out: "I see ships lying!" and he counted twenty-three of them. Hearing that we sprang up for joy. Then speedily put out the oars and rowed that way, for it was (as related) calm.

Had we not found these ships here, we should have sailed on to Bantam, where we should have been caught in a trap, for they were at war with our nation[3], the which was a remarkable providence of God for us. We thanked the Lord for His goodness in this matter.

These were all Dutch ships; their commander was of Alkmaar, named Frederik Houtman[4]. He stood at that time in the gallery looking through his telescope or glass towards us, being much amazed at our marvellous sails, not knowing who it was. He sent out his pinnace which rowed towards us to see what kind of folk we were. On coming together we looked and at once knew one another, for we had sailed with them out of Texel and had lost sight of one another in the Spanish sea outside the Channel. The Merchant and I went over into their sloop and rowed to Houtman's ship named *de Maeght van Dordrecht*[1]. The commander Houtman called us aft into the cabin, and gave us welcome, he let the table be spread for us to eat with him. But when I saw the bread and other food, my heart failed and my stomach closed up and tears of joy ran down my cheeks so that I could not eat. Our other men when come on board were speedily divided among the ships.

Houtman at once ordered a pinnace to take me and the Merchant to Batavia. And after we had related to him all our adventures and misfortunes, we went into the pinnace and set sail. We came the next morning before the town of Batavia.[2] The men we knew on the ships had already supplied us with Indian clothes so that we were in good trim before we came into the town.

We went into the town and came before the House where the Governor-General Jan Pietersz Coen of Hoorn resided. We begged the halbardiers to make inquiry if we might go to the General, for we would have speech with him. They went within and returned, and we were admitted and came to him. He knew nought of our arrival, but bade us welcome when we gave our names. Then we had to make a clean breast of it and we said; "Sir General, at such a time we sailed from Texel with the ship *New Hoorn*, and at such a time we reached the strait of Sunda, and in such a degree there befel us the disaster that our ship was set on fire and blown to pieces." And we related to him bit by bit how and by what means it came about and that I myself was blown up with the ship, yet by God's mercy was saved, as also another young man; and I am preserved to this day, the Lord be praised. Hearing this the General said, "That can't be helped; it is a great misfortune". He questioned us as to all our happenings, and we told him everything just as it had taken place. And he said again: "That can't be helped, it is a great misfortune" After that he said: "Boy, bring me the golden cup". This he caused to be filled with Spanish wine and said: "Good luck, Captain, here's to you! You may well think that your life had been lost and that God Almighty has restored it to you again. Stay here and eat at my table for I intend this night to set out for Bantam, to the ships, to make certain arrangements. Remain here until I send for you or return here myself". Then he drank to the Merchant as well, and we had more discourse. At last he departed, and we stayed there and ate at his table the space of eight days. He then summoned us again to come to him at Bantam in the ship *de Meaght van Dordrecht*, where we had been before, and he sent for me first and said: "Captain Bontekoe, you are placed provisionally, till further order, on the ship the *Berger-Boot*[1] to under take the duty of Captain as you have done before". I said: "I thank the Lord General for this favour".

Two or three days later he sent for the Merchant Heyn Rol and said: "Merchant, you are sent provisionally, till further order, to the ship *Berger-Boot* to be supercargo thereon such as you have been before". Thus we were together again and in command of a vessel.

The *Berger-Boot* was a short ship with thirty-two pieces, and appeared to be full of cannon mostly two tiers high. We sailed in the first part of the year 1620 to Ternate[1], our ship loaded with meat, bacon and rice, also much ammunition of war to supply the forts there; we were three ships in all, to wit: the *Berger-Boot* on which I was, the *Neptune*, and the *Morghenstar*; we touched at Gresse[2] on the way. A chief merchant, Wolter Hudden, of Riga in Livland, who was in charge there brought us on board many cattle, fowls, geese, arack, and black sugar. The food for the beasts was rice but half-grown, so as it had been cut off the land, and called paddhi. We put off again from Gresse sailed along the coast past the strait of Bali, as far as the land of Solor[3] to get the wind, for the Monsoon was passed; so doing we hoped to come the easier to Ambony. But when we came before the harbour of Solor, there came on board the Merchant of the fort, one Raemburgh of Enckhuysen, who had his residency there, and told us that there was a place near to named Larantoeka[1], from where the Specks[2] and Mestizzos who lived there did much damage to our trade, and said it was now a good occasion (while we were three together) to attack the aforementioned place. Whereupon we resolved to undertake this. We sailed thither, accompanied by several Corracorras[3] and a large number of vessels of the country that came to see the event of the affair but came not to help therein. We ran under the fort and the hamlet and shot lustily at them and they likewise at us. At the same time we landed our men, but those of the town made two or three assaults and drove our men back, so that some twenty or twenty-five of our men fell and many were wounded. We were thus forced to return having achieved nothing. We fetched water and took leave of the chief merchant Raemburgh and set our course to N.E. to sail above the island of Batamboer; had sight of it and left it on our larboard; set our course then North East by North to sail the islands of Boeroe and Blau[4], which we left also to larboard of us. We ran then to the island of Amboina, but could not make it, being thrown out of our course by the current. We got below it, between two small islands, into an inlet named Hieto[5], and over against it lay Combello where there are many cloves.

From Hieto a man on horseback can in a short time

ride to Amboina[1]. We found there three commanders, to wit: the governor Houtman of Alkmaar, the governor 'tLam of Hoorn, with governor Speult. Het Lam had his residency on Maleyen[2], governor Speult on Amboina[3], and Houtman was destined to go with us to Batjan[4], where we arrived. And after lying there four or five days, we took leave. The chief merchant of the fort was relieved, his time being expired, and our Merchant Heyn Rol put in his place. Next we went on to all forts in the Moluccas and provided them with meat, bacon, rice, oil, vinegar and other necessaries. We lay at the island of Maleyen (where the governor Jan Dirckz 'tLam had his residency), about three weeks; took leave of 'tLam and returned to Batjan, where we (as related) had left our merchant Heyn Rol, who had command of the fort. He gave us about 200 tons of cloves.

Here I took my leave of Heyn Rol, the tears ran down our cheeks, it cut us both to the heart, after we had endured so much misery and peril together as before related. Since that time I saw him never again, but I have been told that some time after this he died and was buried on the island of Maleyen. The Lord have mercy on his soul and on mine when my time comes.

We than sailed across the Boggeronis or Strait of Boeton.[5] Ran through the Boggeronis, then across to sail above the shoals ſtraight to Java Minor or Little Java[1] and so along the coaſt to Gresse. On coming to Gresse we loaded as many bullocks and fowls as we could put in, in number about ninety beaſts and sixteen hundred fowls, with some geese and ducks. We gave them paddhi for food. Sixteen fowls could be had there for a real of eight. Took leave again of the merchant Wolter Hudden and set our course along Java. We sailed close by Japara but did not touch it; continued our journey and came safely to Batavia.

Here we spoke again with the General Coen of Hoorn. Unloaded our ship. That done I was sent with the same ship to Jambi, to fetch from there a shipload of pepper. On the way touched at Palembang. Brought a shipload of pepper to Batavia.

Then the General sent me to the islands that lie off the route from Bantam to Batavia[2] to fetch ſtone that lies there on the ground. They gave me forty lascars to drive and faſten them to the ropes so as to haul them into the boat. These are large ſtones which they know how to hew into blocks in Batavia, and they finish the points of the fort therewith. This ſtone is very white, far whiter than lime ſtone in Holland. The fort is built moſtly of such ſtone, right out of the water to the top; a pleasure to look at. We made three such voyages for ſtone. Then came the ship *Groningen* from home, of which Tobias Emden was Captain, and

Mr van Neck, who had been sheriff at Texel, Merchant. And seeing that the Captain and the Merchant had not been able to live in accord together, they were both by order of our General Coen and his Council put on to the *Berger-Boot*, and I on to the ship *Groningen* with a Junior Merchant given me, by name Jan Claesz of Amsterdam.

It was no bad change for me, for on the *Berger-Boot* the kitchen was as bare as a board, as the saying is, and the ship *Groningen* was just come from Holland and had plenty of everything. I was ordered to go with it to Jambi again for pepper, with two chests of money; we should touch at Palembang in passing, which we did and found there a Merchant of Alkmaer, named Hooghlandt. We left a chest of money with him and set on further to Jambi. At that place was a Merchant of Delft, by name Abraham van der Dussen, for whom we brought also a chest of money. We lay there long in the road; our lading was brought on board by small boats, besides that we with our own boat rowed off and on every day to fetch pepper from the river. Our chief mate Sipke of Enchyusen, went with the sloop all the way up to the Merchant and found the bark *de Bruynvis*[1] lying by the town, whereof was captain Jaep Mertsz of Hoorn; and after he had made good cheer there in the evening he went to sleep on the afterdeck and rolled off with the blanket round him into the water and was drowned, at which tiding I was much grieved. When we had the lading aboard, we took leave of Mr van der Dussen and returned to Batavia; there at once unloaded our ship; we then made again two journeys for stone to the above-named islands. That being done, we sailed again to Jambi for pepper, on which journey our supercargo Jan Claesz died; we then returned to Batavia.

With these voyages in the *Berger-Boot* as also the *Groningen* I was busied some two years. It was then resolved that with this same ship I should go to China in company with seven more ships under Commander Cornelis Reyersz of Gouda, with intent, were it possible, to capture the town of Macao[1], or to go to the Pescadores and try all possible means to establish a trade with the Chinese, all of which was expressed more fully in the instructions given us by the Governor-General Coen. The General to that end had sent letters to many places ordering the ships to join us at such and such points which we should pass. Among others also to the Manillas[2] to Commander Willem Jansz, who with some Englishmen, was there on an expedition, that some of his ships should join us, which also took place.

The 10th April (1622) after we had lain for some time before Batavia, we set sail, being eight ships; set our course to go through the Strait of Balimbam.[3]

The 11th we had sight of the land of Sumatra. We here fell more southwards than we reckoned, by which we surmised the current ran out of the Strait of Sunda.

The 12th, 13th, 14th and 15th we had variable wind and weather, passed the island of Lucipara.

The 16th and 17th we reached the island of Banka.

The 18th we met with the ship *Nieuw Zealandt* coming out of Japan, which had with her two Portuguese sloops taken by our ships before Malacca, going to Batavia.

The 19th to 25th we made little progress, the wind and current being mostly against us, so that we must often come to anchor.

The 29th in the afternoon we came to the northern end of the Strait of Balimbam, and the island of Banka was S.E. of us at about a mile distant ; we continued north to the island of Polepon[1].

The 30th we came to anchor at the S.E. end of Polepon in twelve fathom and sandy ground. Its coast is highland.

The 1st May we lay to the West side of the aforenamed island in nineteen fathom anchor ground over against the most northerly sand-bay, where the fresh water is a little within the wood, in a flat hollow or dell. From the north end of the island of Banka to this above-mentioned island the course is North nineteen miles.

The same day we set sail again; set our course N.E. and N.E. by N., so as to sail above or to the east of the island of Linga.

The 2nd we kept twelve miles N.E. by N. After noon the east corner of the island of Linga was four miles S.W. by W. of us. The coast is very high on the north side. From the west side of Polepon to the east side or corner of Linga the course is N.N.E. and so northerly nine miles, depth eighteen, nineteen, twenty fathom.

The 3rd the island of Polepaniang[1] was W. and W. by S. of us.

The 4th we took our height and found 1 degree 48 minutes north of the Æquinoctial Line. In the afternoon we had sight of the island of Laur, about eight miles N.W. of us the coast high, rising like a lofty mountain, deep thirty-five fathom.

The 6th the island of Pole Timon was W. of us about six miles; set our course N.N.E. to the island of Pole Candore.[2]

The 9th orders were given for us, with three ships, to go forward, to the island Pole Cecir, to wit: the ship *Groningen* (on which I was), *de Engelsche Beer* and *St. Nicolaes*.

The 18th in the morning we had sight of the island of Pole Candore N.N.E. of us about nine miles; it is a high coast with small islands lying for the most part on the S.E. side of the large island. The watering-place is on the S.W. side. From the island of Pole Timon to this island the course is straight N.N.E. following the charts; in the waterway deep thirty-five, forty, fifty, sixty fathom, soft ground, but coming near to Pole Candore you find again thirty, twenty-five, twenty fathom, hard sand. In the evening we sailed close round the east of the island, about a good half-mile from the most easterly islet; deep eighteen and twenty fathom. We set our course to N.E. for the coast of Champey.[1]

The 21st in the evening, we could still see Pole Candore from the main topmast.

The 22nd we had sight of the coast of Champey.[1]. When you are about seven or eight miles from the land, it appears as if it were islands.

The 24th we had sight of our other ships again, being at the height of 10 degrees 35 minutes; we were about one and a half miles from the land; the shore here is low, of white sand, but the interior of the land is high and hilly. Along the coast, one, two, three miles to sea, it is deep seventeen, sixteen, fifteen, fourteen, thirteen fathom and sand. At evening we came to anchor all together in fifteen fathom under a point or corner named Cape of Cecir, being in the height of 10¾ degrees. To the north of this cape there is a large bay, where further along the shore is duneland, the inland country very high and mountainous. The coaſt, from this cape, runs N.E. by E.

The 25th we were close to the islet with the cliffs of ſtone, named Pole Cecir de Terre. Here on the north of the land there is an inlet which runs into the high ground like a river. The dune coaſt here comes to an end, and there follows high land with deeper water, thirty, forty, and fifty fathom.

The 26th we came to anchor in Malle Bay (by the inhabitants called Bay of Paderan). Here our chief mate Abram Thysz of Flushing went over to the ship *St. Nicolaes*, bound for the Manillas, to see if he could find some ships of Willem Jansz's fleet. There are here many high palm trees by the houses along the shore.

The next day we sailed with our four ships to another bay called Canberine[1], about six miles further and found here water and wood in plenty, as also refreshment in abundance. We got some seventeen oxen and a good number of fowls ; but a Speck of ours deserting to the inhabitants we could obtain no more refreshing afterwards.

The 4th June I went with the boat to our companions in the Bay of Paderan, to report to them of our adventures and returned on the 6th day of that month. Meanwhile the sloop *St. Cruys* had come to us. The next day we set sail and came to the sloop *de Haan*,[2] which had captured a Japanese junk, and there by our own ships.

The 10th we saw a small island that lay under the coast in shape like the Coxbroad by England.

The 20th having sighted several islands on our way, we saw two sails close under the coast. At evening we came to overtake the ships to the Manillas, *de Hoop*[1] with *The Bull*, that was an Englishman; kept near them all night.

The 22nd we came to Macao and let anchor fall in four fathom soft ground; we were then fifteen sail strong, ships and sloops, among them two English ships.

We had a roll-call of our men, and had them to exercise round the mast, in which they were instructed according to the use of war. The same they did on the other ships.

The 23rd, afternoon, with three of our ships, to wit: *Groningen*, *de Galias* and *de Engelsche Beer*, we came close up to the town and anchored in three fathom at low tide, about a pedereo-shot from the shore, we shot that evening therein five shots. In the night two of us, to wit: *Groningen* and *de Galias*, came to the distance of a little more than a musket-shot before the town in three fathom, half flood-tide and soft ground.

It was agreed that I and our Merchant Bosschert, of Delft, with our men, should row to land and help to storm the town, but this resolution was changed, so as not to deprive the ship of Captain and Merchant at the same time, and I was to stay on the ship and look to affairs, and our Commander go as Captain of the force on land.

In the morning, being the 24th day, at break of day we shot into the town with all our broadsides that it shook, as much shot as the pieces could bear. A short time after, the Commander Cornelis Reyersz landed with about six hundred men able to bear arms. Two sloops ran close in shore where the Commander landed, so that in case it went ill with our men they could retreat into them and also to protect the boats and small vessels. The Portuguese had thrown up a breast-work at the spot where our men were to land, from that they offered some resistance, but when our men pressed forward, they fled up the slope to a monastery. Being on land our men advanced valiantly on the Portuguese, who made several sallies against us, but were driven back continually with great courage. Then by mischance some half-barrels of powder got afire which placed our men in a quandary, for before any other could be brought, the Portuguese were acquainted thereof by some Japanese deserters. Our men minding to draw off, the Portuguese on that afore-mentioned report came and fell on them, and as they, through want of powder, could not sufficiently defend themselves, many were slain. The rest retired in much confusion into the boats and came on board. We reckoned to have loſt 130 men in all, and had also as many injured; among them the Commander Cornelis Reyersz, who when firſt our men landed, was shot in the belly, but by God's help he was cured of his hurt.

The men again on board, we sailed off about three-quarters of a mile and fetched water from an island south of Macao. We took in again our chief mate who had been formerly put off.

The 27th day, departed the two English ships with the ship *de Trou*[1] to Japan. The ship *de Hoop* was also placed under our flag.

The 28th day *de Beer* and *St. Cruys* sailed to the island of Lemon[2] and further to inspect the coaſt of China.

The 29th day we all set sail for the Pescadores, save the ship *de Hoop*, the sloop *St. Nicolaes* and the small sloop *Palicatten*[3], which were to ſtay there till the end of Auguſt to watch for the ships that might come there from Malacca.[4]

The 30th we passed Idelemo, otherwise the Hare's Ears, ran eaſt and E. by S. to go above Pole or Pedro Blanco, the islet looks from far like to a large ship or Caravel.

The 4th July from our top we had sight of the island of the Pescadores.

The 6th day the ship *de Beer* came again to us from

the coast of China, we held together round the outside of the islands.

The 10th we came to anchor behind one of the islands; it rises like a table and was one of the highest islands of the Pescadores. We saw between the islands some Chinese fishermen, but they fled before us.

The next day we weighed anchor and ran into a fine enclosed bay, in eight or nine fathom anchorage. This country is flat and stony, has no trees from which to get wood, is grown over with long grass; it has reasonably fresh water to be got from wells, but the weather being dry it is brackish. The water is found in two inlets where the ships lie; otherwise here is no refreshment, it must all be brought there, and as this place was appointed to us for a rendezvous, we put in to a harbour at the end of Ile Formosa, named Tayowan[1] where the Chinese have some trade. From there we afterwards, with our sloops, fetched much victual; it lies thirteen miles from the Pescadores, has no more than eleven foot of water at the entrance, which is somewhat crooked, so that large vessels cannot come into it.

The 19th day we sailed, namely the ship *Groningen* and *de Beer*, to go over to the coast of China; we met with the sloop *St. Cruys*. The next day *de Beer* broke her foreyard by reason of which we were forced to take in sail to keep in company with her.

The 21st we had sight of the continent of China and came before the renowned river Chinchu[1]. This river is easily recognisable, for such as Jan Huygen van Linschoten doth relate[2]: at the corner on the N.E. side are two hills, one of which is like the pillar of a church, and the S.W. side of the river is low, sandy ground, and a little to the inside of the S.W. corner can be seen a tower or what has the likeness thereof. Here we should have run on the S.W. side under a small round island, but as the ship *de Beer* could not make the road, we had to stand out to sea again, for her broken yard was not yet repaired. It now began to blow hard, so that the next day our foresail blew out of the bolt-ropes; we beat up against the wind, but were driven strongly to the north.

The 25th we sighted a very broken coast at the height of 27 degrees 9 minutes, which we surmised both by the writing of Jan Huygen and by the showing of the chart, to be in the island of Lanquyn. Came to anchor under it in fifteen fathom; we saw many Chinese fishermen, about three, four, five to six miles out from land.

We did every day our utmost to steer south but were driven continually northward, from which it appears there goes a strong northerly current.

The 27th came a fisherman alongside of us who sold us some dried fish.

The 9th August we found ourselves by the islands

of China, which are very numerous. Came to anchor in fifteen fathom. Judging by the chart, and the height we took, we did conjecture to be about the Cape de Somber, but could not see either cape nor coast, therefore judged the cape to be more northerly than shown by the charts.

The 11th we weighed anchor and ran under the island of Lanquyn, that lies in 28½ degrees north of the Æquinoctial Line, in a tolerable road on the north side of which we had discovered with the boat, to seek water and refreshment; found none or scanty victuals, but there was good water. As we lay here there came to us some Chinese in their sampan, who presented us with five baskets of white sugar for each ship. They were we surmised, so far as we could understand from them, Chinese pirates, freebooters on their own nation. The next day we fetched our water and set sail again, but prospered little.

The 18th day we cast anchor again on the west side of the same island in a better road than the other; it was a harbour where one is sheltered from nearly all winds. Here the aforesaid pirates had their anchorage, they brought us some victual which they knew where to find, but it was of little use for the whole of our ships' crews. They many times proposed that we should go with them to the coast and so they might be in our shelter, they would bring refreshment for us, yea, boat-loads thereof, yet we thought it not advisable to do this. They hoisted Prince-flags[1] on their little ships and under that ensign robbed their own nation.

We set sail again to join our other ships in the Pescadores, where after much variable weather we arrived on the 22nd September. There we saw our men at work to throw up a fort or castle. We found also two ships with a sloop more than we had left there, come later from Batavia, to wit: the ship *de Gouden Leeuw*[2], the *Sampson* and the sloop *Sincka-Pure.*[3]

The next day there came two sloops from the coast of China, having left one behind that was wrecked on that coast, but they had saved the men and the guns; in this the Chinese had been very helpful to them. These ships had been sent out to talk with the Chinese for traffic; who sent them back with great expectations and did promise to come to us with an ambassador in the Pescadores to speak further together, which on the 29th day they did. They came with four junks with their ambassador, to agree with our commander and council about the traffic, but nothing was carried out; for all they promised they kept not, seeking by these means to move us from the Pescadores, the which was contrary to the orders given us by our Governor-General.

The 10th October *de Gouden Leeuw* set sail to Jambi.

The 18th day we, namely eight sail, three ships and

five sloops, were ordered to go to the river Chinchu and the coast of China to see if through fear of our enmity and force we could more them to traffic with us,[1] but we came about ten miles too low. Three of our ships were parted from us; we were then five, and cast anchor in a bay where by our sloops we set afire as much as sixty or seventy junks great and small.[2]

There here befel an affair worthy to be recorded. As our men were busied in bringing two junks they had seized alongside of us, and by reason of the strong wind were forced to anchor, having with them the boat with our pinnace, in the forepart of the night their anchors slipped and they drifted away, the one having in her twenty-three of our men and two Chinese. The sloop *Victoria* that lay anchored beside them to help them, by reason of the foul weather and darkness could give no assistance. The one junk drifted away, those in the other junk, who were six, removed into the boat and set fire to the junk, but as they could hardly put up sail in the boat, and being on a low shore, they threw out the grapnel. But after lying about two hours with the grapnel the rope broke and they were driven onto the shore in peril of their lives, and more so because in being beached the matches of their muskets were blown out, and they had nothing but enemies to expect on land, and were too few in number to resist force; for they were but four men and two boys. Therefore they gave up the matter to God and prayed to Him to deliver them from their peril. Thus they sat in great fear and trembling in the boat and waited for daybreak. Presently there came a body of Chinese to the boat. Our men grasped their swords in their hands and shouted and cried as if they would attack them. Hearing which the Chinese, who by reason of the darkness could not see how many men there were, made away, as it were, afraid of the affrighted. Our men took this for a certain token of God's mercy and protection over them. When day came they resolved to leave the boat (seeing it was impossible for them to bring her off the shore into the water), with muskets on their shoulders and swords at their sides, were it possible, to journey by land to the river of Sammitju before which our two sloops lay. The twenty-three men who had drifted away with the other junk, were captured. Some years later one of the twenty-three men came back as I have heard. But these six could see no junk or any sign of it being on shore; therefore they marched on.

A body of Chinese seeing them, came to them and sent two of their men forward to speak with ours; but our men trusted them not and lifted their matches as if to shoot at them, upon which they let them pass.

Finding a small house wherein was a man and woman, on their way, they went therein, lighted their matches and put their guns in order, which were altogether unready by reason of being wetted in landing with the boat. Here too they had food, for this man gave them some rice, and thanking him they haſtened on they way. They saw some six or seven Chinese lie dead on the shore, a prey for the dogs and birds ; they had been slain by our men. From this they could judge easily what would be done to them if they were taken ; they resolved therefore to defend themselves so long as they could hold a sword in their hands.

After this they met with a multitude of Chinese, they thought as many as two hundred, who all fled from them. In the afternoon they came near our sloops, and fired several shots with their muskets so as to be heard and fetched by those in the sloops. But by reason of the shots there came seven or eight hundred Chinese (as they eſtimated) running out of a large village nearby ; they came towards our men armed with knives and pikes. Our men (as it seemed) had nothing but death before them, sent some shots among the crowd. Seeing that our men were resolved to die fighting, they ran back ; some came to a ſtand afar off and threw ſtones ; it appeared they had not heard much shooting, for they were mightily shaken thereat our men said. Then after awhile they offered them friendship ; and asked them to come to their village.

Being come into the village there ſtood some thousand

Chinese (at a guess) who gazed at them with wonder; it seemed they had never yet looked upon any Hollander in their lives. They brought our men into their temple; gave them food and drink and some tobacco. Our men sat down close together, their guns held ready for they trusted no one and feared they would be surprised. Sitting thus their match was burnt; they tore pieces from their shirts and twisted them into a match as well as they could. They then went away from the village thanking the Chinese for the benefit received, rejoicing to escape so happily from there, and that no one pursued them, for they had not four shots of powder left in their bandoleers.

They came to the beach, found there a sampan, and pushed off. Coming into the water it sank immediately it was so leaky. They then went into a fisherman's house where some of them lay down to sleep, but the others could not or dared not sleep as they heard in the night a party of Chinese round the house. In the morning they made two rafts of what they could find best suited to the purpose, and came therewith to the sloops which were about to sail, so that they must not have been any longer about it or they would have been left behind. By these happenings it can be seen clearly what perils a man can come through if the Lord's protection works mercifully for him, for without that it were almost a miracle that so small a band of men should have escaped out of the hands of the Chinese, who were their enemies.

The 2nd November the sloop *St. Nicolaes* sailed to the place where the boat lay ashore; it had been plundered by the Chinese of its sails, maſt, rudder, two small guns and the iron plate from the prow. They set it afloat and brought away ten goats and three or four pigs by way of reprisals, and so with the boat to the ship.

The 4th day *de Beer's* boat took two junks with twenty-five men and set the junks afire, the men they brought to the sloop *St. Nicolaes*.

The 9th November our chief mate died at sea, we buried him on an island in 23 degrees.

The same day the boat of *de Beer* sailed to a party of junks, but the wind came so ſtrong that the abovementioned boat with eighteen men, among them the captain Jan Jansz, drifted away, to the great grief of all of us. We sent the sloop *Victoria* to seek her, but had never sight of her again. Lying here with our two ships, we had loſt forty of our beſt sailors, which grieved us mightily.

The 25th we came together before the river Chinchu. Caſt anchor under an island by a town, from which the inhabitants took flight. We brought therefrom about forty beaſts, among which several pigs; also a number of hens, which served well for refreshing, as many of our men lay ill and were much revived by these victuals.

We sent three sloops into the river, which came to anchor by a village where they landed and skirmished lustily against the Chinese.[1] The Chinese fastened nine junks together, set them on fire and let them drift towards our sloops meaning to set them afire, but they missed them. We came with our two ships the 28th of the same month, and there shot with our gig ordnance at a place from where with seven small cannon they had shot at the men from our sloops, who bravely held their ground though they were but fifty in number and the Chinese some thousand strong. They drew off their canon a space from their village. Our men set afire four junks before the village and came aboard again in the evening.

The 29th day there came a Chinese deserter but he seemed to be half-mad. We weighed anchor and came before a town, and shot at it, they likewise with their small cannon at us, and touched us twice. We set a junk on fire. *De Beer* with a sloop ran to the other side of the island; they saw there two large villages, and next to the one two large junks on the stocks. We resolved to raid this, which we undertook the 30th with about seventy musketeers.

The inhabitants were all fled to a certain fort, we pursued them up to the fort. They made two sallies with such horrid cries and screaming as if the end of the world were come; they came at us lustily and we not willing to give way, we did beat our swords about one another's heads. But when we had shot down a number of them with our muskets they fell back and took to their heels. They had beaten down our sergeant and the sailmaker of *de Beer*, who if we had not relieved them would have been dead. The sergeant's bandoleer was cut off his body. We drove them back to their fort, slaying them all the while. We lost one man; he was the barber of *de Beer*, but if he were slain or taken prisoner we knew not. We set the two junks as well as their whole village on fire and came again on board at evening with a good booty of pigs, goats, hens and other plunder, pieces of furniture and various things. The beasts we made ready that night to make good cheer next day, after this difficult enterprise on land.

The 2nd December we went again on land and plundered another village, set it afire as the previous one. We found here twenty-one bales of twisted silk thread in a warehouse and brought it with the other booty on board.

The next day we sailed to another island, on which stood a great tower. We found no people there; cast anchor at high water in 5½ fathom and in the early part of the night with low tide we found ourselves fast;

it appeared that a powerful current goes here in and out. That same night with the flood tide, the Chinese sent two fire junks at us, they drifted near *de Beer*, which lay at anchor above us. One of them seemed about to come ſtraight for our bow, which caused great conſternation in our ship. We ſtood all men on deck and some said this and some said that. But I making sure that it would miss us was not so diſtressed. The Merchant Nieuwenrode who ſtood near me said: "Captain, let them cut the rope". I informed him that it was not advisable to cut the rope while we lay on the shore; it would of necessity lose us our ship and that the junk would not touch us. But the junk nearing us, the merchant judged it could not miss, he cried out: "Cut the rope! Cut the rope!" And I shouted againſt him: "Don't cut, for if you cut we shall lose the ship. It will miss us, don't cut!" When the Merchant saw that the men who had already begin to cut the rope ſtayed their hand and liſtened to me, he called to me (believing the junk to be as good as aboard us): "Captain Bontekoe, see, it is your fault. I shall make you suffer for this". But I ſtill in fear that the men should cut through the rope, called again: "'Twill miss, 'twill miss, don't cut, don't cut!" Which was truth, for it gave us so wide a berth that it even missed our mainyard which was then athwart, although its maſt was much higher than our yard. Only our sampan that lay alongside our ſtern, did catch fire, which we cut adrift, so certainly it was a good thing it did not come much closer. It was an awful sight, for the junk burned so mightily as if it had been filled with sulphur, and would have made short work of us. I had the rudder moved over from one side to the other, which had made the ship swing from the anchor, which (next God) was the only cause that the junk missed us.

The 4th we weighed anchor and came to the island in the mouth of the river from where we had taken the forty beaſts, as related. We there fetched water and set sail from there the 7th day to go across to the Pescadores. Being halfway over our fore-mainsail was blown away, and the next day we caſt anchor (by reason of the intemperate weather we could not use sail to go inside the inlet before which we ſtood) under the next island that lies to the weſt of the inlet, in fifteen fathom.

The 9th day we broke from our anchorage, dropped another anchor, but after lying four hours the rope of this broke also. We then drifted away from the islands and that in a violent storm from N.E. and N.N.E.

The 10th our ship did so leak that with two pumps it was as much as we could do to keep above water, we had seven foot water in the ship and our ſtern pump was every now and again out of order. We had aft in the storehouse a load of paddhi and when a hole was sprung in the storehouse, the paddhi slipped down it into the pump, which made our pump almost useless, as stated. We were therefore forced to throw the paddhi overboard for we feared that it would fill up the scuppers and make them useless.

The 13th and 14th it became good sailing weather; we found ourselves close under the coast of China; we here met the ship *Haerlem*, whereof my brother Pieter Ysbrantsz Bontekoe was captain, they also had intended to be at the Pescadores and were driven away by the aforesaid storm; they came from Japan. We held together four days, but we lost more way than we gained; therefore ran together into the roadstead on the coast of China.

The 20th the ship *Haerlem* took some seven sampans with thirty-six Chinese in them and three junks that were loaded with salt, salted fish and other goods. The same day it was agreed that we should take over the lading brought by the *Haerlem* from Japan; for the ship *Haerlem* was weak and in such case that she dared not put off to have her bottom doubled, and on the other hand our ship was strong and good. Also we were water-tight again. We therefore cleared up our ship and began the next day to load. Then came two Chinese from the land to the ship *Haerlem*; they brought some apples, fowls and pigs on board, for which deed they gave him his junk back. We then here fetched water and made ready to sail again : put up a fish on our foremast and yard.

The 1st January (1623) it was resolved that the chief mate Jan Garritsz de Naeyer with some sixty persons of the ship *Haerlem* should come on our ship. And our second mate Geleyn Cornelisz with others went over to the ship *Haerlem* to go to Batavia and so further home. The Merchants were busy writing letters to that end, the one to Batavia the other to the Pescadores.

We put over some eighty-four Chinese on to the ship *Haerlem* which set sail from us the 4th day to Batavia. In the night the Chinese fetched away a junk from near our ship though we shot at them; they got away ; we had no yawl to pursue them.

The 5th the Chinese came and fished round about us. It seemed they knew we had no yawl, our carpenters were busy every day making one. We had procured a half-worn sail from the ship *Haerlem* and therewith we furnished the yawl and our ship with what was needful. We kept good watch by night being fearful of burning junks the Chinese might send us.

The 7th we set sail for the open sea ; but by reason of contrary winds were forced to return. Came back to our old anchorage, took a junk as we were sailing, from which we took the cables and other rope-work and then set it on fire. The men had fled out of it; the rope-work came in very handy to us.

The 9th and 10th we finished the maſt, wings and other gear of our yawl; were ſtill held in the road by unfavourable wind.

The 11th day we saw towards evening two junks under the shore. The Merchant desired we should send the boat to them, but I deemed it not advisable, for the night drew near and the weather was very tempeſtuous, it showed as if to blow harder, and looked evil. So I said that we ought not to risk our men lightly; therefore it was not done. By night there rose a ſtorm and we were right glad the boat had remained on board.

The next day, in the morning, we went with the boat to a junk which came tacking into the bay; but ere we could get up to it there came four war-junks to its assiſtance who shot mightily at us and as it was close to land where there ſtood as much as a thousand people (so it seemed) on the beach, armed, we were forced to leave it and return on board.

The 14th, at night in the firſt watch, I went with the boat to another junk, which put up a fight and shot for about two glasses at us, and seeing we drifted too far from the ship and had but little chance to take the junk, we came back on board in the day-watch.

The 15th the chief mate with the boat went out again to a junk that came from Teysing; they attacked it lustily but were forced to leave it. They had three wounded among them, one fatally, for he was shot through by a poisoned weapon.

The 18th I went with the boat to five junks, one held on its way and the other four roped themselves together side by side and made ready for a fight with shields, swords, arrows and small cannon—for they were war junks—so that after but little fighting we left them. The junks came after us. Our men in the ship seeing this, and being in fear they would seize us, made ready our two stern guns to shoot at them, for it was near the ship; we were not a thousand steps from the ship. We furled the sail and lowered the foresail and rowed right up against the wind. Those in the junks seeing this turned away from us. In the evening we came on board again and set sail that same night with the wind N.W

The 19th in the morning we were about a mile outside the coast or from the point of Teysing; we had Peter Blanca S.E. of us about five miles; it lies in the height of 22 degrees 20 minutes; we sailed along the coast. On the same day we gave rations to the crew, one tankard of water a day.

The 20th by sundown, on account of contrary winds, we cast anchor again in seventeen fathom about six miles from land, N. by E. from Cache, for we could gain no way by sailing. Here our cable broke, so we were forced to hoist sails again, yet next day through ill weather we came again to anchor about eight miles eastward of Teysing.

The 22nd we sent out the boat nearer land to seek for better anchorage; on their report we sailed up within half a cannon shot off the shore, in a good roadstead.

The 23rd in the morning, wind still continued contrary from N.E. with cool weather.

The 24th died the man who was so grievously wounded nine days earlier, named Hendrick Bruys, of Bremen.

The 25th our carpenters had the pinnace near finished.

The 27th our Merchant Nieuwenroode sailed to land with the yawl and longboat, to see if water was to be found, but there was none. We saw some junks lying in the river and in the afternoon we attacked them with muskets; but they shot at us with small cannon and hoisted sail, so we came back having done them no hurt.

The 28th our chief mate took a small junk with dried and salted fish, and eight Chinese, who yielded themselves at once.

The 29th and 30th we made several attacks on junks

and fisher-boats, but took only one fisher-boat with five men. We sought for water which I did find the 31st day, very sweet and fresh and easy to come at.

The following days to the 7th February we took in water; every day it was foul and variable weather with wind contrary for continuing our voyage.

The 8th we went with the boat and yawl and twenty-seven musketeers to land to make an expedition. We came to a village from which the people were fled; marched inland a short way and found a herd of buffaloes, of which we brought seventeen to the ship with four pigs and many hens. It was every day foul weather.

The 10th day the Merchant Niewenroode went again with yawl and boat on land and twenty-five musketeers; they marched inland; came to two villages from which the people were all fled; set on fire both villages and came again on board.

The 11th day one of our two small junks turned over and sank, but the mast which was fourteen palm thick and 59 ft. long, we managed to get out. Out boat went again to land to fetch straw for the buffaloes.

The 12th we made another land raid with fifty armed men. Plundered two villages, saw some buffaloes but could not catch them; took some sacks of garlic and onions, and after being some two miles inland returned on board.

The 15th our chief mate was put in irons, for reason of there being fire in his cabin, but was released at evening. Our carpenters made a fishplate on our main-mast.

The 18th we put overboard a man who had died the night before. We most days made expeditions with our small junk or yawl or boat to the fishing vessels and junks, but could gain nothing. It was mostly foul weather and cold.

The 20th we took a junk with fourteen Chinese. They told us they came out of the river Chinchu, also that Commander Cornelis Reyersz had made a treaty with the people of Chinchu, but all the same we took it and put the goods over into our ship. We repaired our mast and bowsprit with fishplates and what was needful.

The 10th March fetched water every day if fair weather. On this day a bird was shot (as he flew in the air) from our ship.

The 14th went on land near all of us, pulled our boat up on shore to caulk and clean it; came on board again in the evening.

The 17th day there died one of the sailors, by name Claes Cornelisz, of Middelburg.

The 18th very intemperate weather with thunder, lightning and rain. This night died the second mate Jan Gerritsz Brouwer of Haarlem, who was made second mate about five and a half weeks before.

The 20th, in the night three Chinese sprang overboard; meaning to get away with the boat, but as the watch became aware of it, we took the one back but the other two were drowned.

The 30th we took two junks and a fishing boat with twenty-seven men.

The 2nd April we put on shore two Chinese who promised to bring us refreshment for their ransom; one was wounded and the other very old.

The 5th we saw two Chinamen stand in our wood-junk and call out to be taken on board. We sent our sampan to them; found one was the same as we had put ashore the 2nd day. They had been brought in the night to our wood-junk by other Chinese and had with them hens, eggs, a pig, lemons, apples, sugar cane and tobacco, some of everything; out of gratitude for having their liberty restored to them. Verily a great virtue, putting to shame many Christians, who once they are out of the trap often think little of their promises.

The 6th we resolved to break up the one junk and lade the timber of it into the other and take it with us to the Pescadores, for they there needed firewood.

The 7th we put the two before-mentioned Chinamen again on land.

The 8th there came a proa to our ship with two other Chinamen, who brought us (like the former) some refreshment, as apples, eggs, some pots of arack, for which we promised to set free two men, one who was wounded, and another, on condition they should bring us more victuals. Gave them also twenty-five reales in money for which to bring us pigs and then allowed them to sail to land. In the night our junk (which we had begun to break up) foundered.

The 9th and 10th we fetched water for the junk as well as for our ship, and put seventeen men of our crew into the junk, to sail together to the Pescadores as soon as wind and weather should be favourable.

The 11th day came the last two Chinamen again from the land bringing with them five pigs, a quantity of eggs, figs, apples and other goods.

The 12th it blew a great storm; we lowered our yards. A Chinese proa was driven away from us with one of our men; sent a yawl and fetched him out; but they could not row back the proa by reason of the great wind; they had bound it to the stern of the yawl, but were forced at last to let it drift and came again on board.

The 13th we let the Chinamen who brought us the refreshment row back to land with their two comrades as promised.

The 15th day the men in the junk were busied in proving a cannon which they had fixed on a new gun-carriage. Charged it with ball-shot; setting its mouth to the door of the junk. Juſt then came a young man out of the hold, and ſtands in the door to make water, knowing nought of the others doing. Then comes one with the lin-ſtock from the other side (not seeing the young man) and puts the fire in and shoots the young man through the leg. Verily a grievous misfortune and very heedless of the rammer.

We slaughtered that afternoon in our ship a buffalo and a pig, for the next day to hold the feaſt of Eaſter.

While they were busied therewith our Dominie fell to scuffling with one of the helpers, both were put in irons.

The 16th being Eaſter Day they were both set free. Then the men from the junk came all into our ship to hear the sermon and ſtayed to dine with us on the buffalo. The next day they came again to hear the preaching ; it was every day tempeſtuous weather and variable winds.

The 19th the young man who was shot in the leg had his leg taken off ; he died about an hour later.

The 20th we had tempeſtuous weather from E.N.E. Lowered our top-maſt, put out another anchor ; it looked as if everything would be blown to pieces. The two Chinamen whom we put off our ship the 13th came again to us and brought some refreshment, told us there would come some two hundred junks together to fall upon us. We therefore made ready (on this warning), so if they came to give them right good greeting.

The 27th we took up our sampan into the ship and set the two fishing proas out of it which the junk took in. We desired to set sail for we dared no longer stay there. But seeing that every day the wind blew a great storm we could not set sail, the more because the wind was against us.

The 28th we put twenty Chinese into the junk, to bring those besides our own to the Pescadores.

The 29th in the morning with better weather, the wind E.N.E., we set sail with our junk, but were much out of our course by the strong contrary wind and other hindrance.

The 1st May, unsettled weather. In the morning we saw that our junk had got away from us, but had sight of her at last a good distance to leeward of us; she lay in distress, her sail was blown away. Resolved as the wind began to grow in force to take the men out of her. To that end I went there with the boat, took the men over; but besides our men, who were sixteen in number, we could not get more than ten Chinese, the others having hid themselves. The wind also became stronger, so that ten Chinese remained in the boat and drifted away. Came in the afternoon on board again; surmised ourselves to be about eight mile outside the easternmost islands of Macao. And as here a steady wind blows from half year to half year that is called Monsoon, so those who come too short of it either on one side or the other of the Pescadores can not well get up to it before the Monsoon changes. For this reason we were here beaten about for a long time, at times riding at anchor, at times sailing, before we could make the Pescadores. We suffered much distress from storm and sickness, for want of refreshing; yea, at last, of ninety men there were not fifty in health of our own crew. On our way we met with another Chinese junk, richly laden to a value of thousands, that was bound for the Manillas. We took it, it had in it as much as 250 souls. Took in most of the men save about twenty or twenty-five and put with them fifteen or sixteen of our own men; we tied the junk to our ship and towed it.

We then had several hundred Chinese in our ship, and feared they might overpower us, for we, as related were but fifty strong of men in health. We caused all our men to go with a sword at their side, as if they were all officers.

By night we let all the Chinese into the hold, then set a beam above on the hatch and hung lamps everywhere about it so that the lower deck was lighted; at the hatch five or six men with bare swords kept watch, and in the morning we opened the hatch and let the Chinese come on deck for needful purposes and other matters; with this our ship was crowded with people. I went often into the cabin to sleep but could not. When I came on deck the Chinese immediately made way for me, went down on their knees on either side with folded hands—they were as lambs. A story was told there was a prophecy among their nation that their land should be conquered by men with red beards, and as I had a red beard, on that account they looked on me with the more fear. Yet this was but what people said; how it is God knows. Nevertheless we durst not trust them.

During the day they sat on the bulwark of the ship and on the chainwales, cleaning and combing their hair. They had such long hair that with many of them when they stood up it hung to the calves of the legs, they twist it like a plait and coil it on their heads, push a pin through to keep it fast, with a comb close to it. We brought them all to the Pescadores; there, with the other Chinese we had brought in other ships and sloops, we tied them together in pairs. We used them to carry earth to the fort, yea, when the fort was built, they were as much as 1,400 in number, who were afterwards taken to Batavia and there sold.[1]

The Pescadores was our rendezvous place, as related and keeping it firmly, went to and fro bringing together there all the Chinese we could take. While we lay here in the Pescadores, we were assailed by such a hurricane of wind that all the ships were nearly blown on the shore ; among them our junk was blown entirely to the land.

There in the Pescadores I had a letter from Batavia, by the hand of Christian Fransz, from my brother Pieter Ysbrantsz Bontekoe, who, as before related, was Captain on the ship *Haerlem*, and on 4th January by the coast of China had left us to go to Batavia. He wrote me that our brother Jacob Ysbrantsz the year before was also come out of Holland as Captain in India, thus we were three brothers in the land, all three Captain. He told that Jacob with the ship *Mauritius* in company with *het Wapen van Rotterdam*, had arrived in distressful condition; they had on the voyage lost about 275 men.[1] *Het Wapen van Rotterdam* had not enough men in health that they could use their sails. Jacob came on two sloops in the Strait of Sunda, that brought him to Batavia, but the other ship, *het Wapen van Rotterdam*, he had left on the south side of Java, whither he was sent with sloops and other vessels to seek her ; he found her and was made Captain of her. He was sent to Amboina. Wrote also that the Governor-General Coen in the ship wherewith Jacob came into this country, that is *Mauritius*, had sailed from the East Indies to Holland the 2nd February 1623, in the company of three other ships, and that Mr Pieter de Carpentier some days before the departure of Mr Coen was made Governor-General of the Indies. There came at that time many families from Holland to Batavia, with *het Wapen van Hoorn* whose captain was Pieter Gerritsz, Bieren-Broots-Pot, and other ships. And many Hollanders were married at Batavia so that many fixed themselves there, not lightly to leave the country.[1]

The 5th October[2], the Commander Cornelis Reyersz and his council[3] ordered us five ships (to wit the ships *Groningen*, *Sampson*, *Muyden*, *Erasmus* and *Victoria*, which last for some reason did not go with us) to go to the river Chinchu, under Commander Christiaen Fransz, to occupy that river so that no junks should sail from there to the Manillas or other places in the hands of our enemies; and as we had often and continually done, to request free trade to Tayowan of them, offering them in that case all peace and friendship; but should they not be willing to consent thereto then to make war on them by water and by land wheresoever the same could take place to the advantage and profit of the Company, such as was more broadly expressed in the instructions given us by the Commander and his council. We set sail this same day.

The 28th we came to the said river, cast our anchor under the island with the pagodas, from where all the people were fled save one old man whom we found. We let fly a white flag (according to our orders) hoping that some one from Amoy would come and speak to us.

The 29th we conferred together and agreed that on each ship we should make ready thirty or forty swabbers and eight or nine tubs of water and also place a number of leather buckets along the ship so that, if the Chinese came to us with fire-junks, we should be able to put them out; as also we should keep strict watch and that every night two pinnace should lie about the third of a mile from the ships to keep watch, also to fetch water. We made the cannon in readiness and were ever on our guard. Then as no one came to us from Amoy, we wrote a letter the 30th day to the Totok[1] of Amoy and sent it by the old Chinaman whom we found on the island. We wrote that we were come there to request of them for traffic and peace so as we had done in the conference held formerly between them and us, with further some compliments befitting this kind of writing. We published also that same day an ordinance on all the ships, impressing on our men the need for keeping good watch, as hostile and treacherous action was to be looked for from the Chinese, and threatening men with severe penalties for neglect of duty.

The 1st November there came a Chinaman named Cipzuan to us with his sampan. He said that if so be we came in peace to request peace and traffic, it would not be their fault if we could not agree, as the inhabitants there were well-inclined, he then gave us hope of good succcess. Said also that some three hundred Chinese merchants had conferred together and resolved to send a request to the Combon of Hockchu[1] petitioning to be allowed to traffic with us since (so he said) by reason of the war they had lost their goods, and should the war continue they were in fear of being brought to poverty altogether; therefore they resolved urgently to beg of the before-mentioned Combon to consent to peace and traffic with us.

This Cipzuan said further that in the place where he lived there was a hermit or anchorite who lived in the mountains; was of high birth and had been mighty rich (I believe also Mardarin over the province) and had withdrawn himself to this solitude after the death of his wife whom he loved dearly; he now busied himself with nought (so he said) but advocating with the great ones the cause of poor people who were without means. Thus he was held in great respect and regard by both great and small; yea, he was esteemed as a prophet and his words accounted to be prophecy. He said also that he had laid before this hermit the differences between us and them, and when understanding that the great ones were preparing to make war on us, he (said Cipzuan) had gone to them and prophesied that (if they did war against us), they would bring their own position into great peril. Upon which

Christiaen Fransz. asked the above-mentioned Cipzuan if he could not have speech with the hermit in order to set forth to him our just and honourable proposals with all circumstance; the which Cipzuan promised to bring about; he doubted not to persuade him and said: "I will do this so that you will believe that I mean well towards you". Thereupon he departed; he declared that he had come to us secretly.

The 3rd day Cipzuan with the said hermit and another Chinaman came on board to us. We related to him the reason of our coming hither and what our intentions and desires were. He (after some speech on both sides) promised to do his utmost to bring the business to a good end. We gave him a letter (of the same contents as that which we had sent by the old Chinaman) for the Totok. He gave his word to hand the same himself to the Totok. Two or three days later Cipzuan came again to us and brought answer to ours, in which the Totok wrote that he understood we had arrived with our ships under the island with the Pagodas to request peace and traffic with them, to the which he would consent if so be we came in good faith and not as we had formerly done, in falsehood and deceit (such he was pleased to write). It would then be possible to come to a good understanding. He had in the last conference with us indicated two ways, to wit: To set free the Chinese prisoners, and go away from Pehoue, called by us the Pescadores; but we had not been willing to accept either of these terms whereby the negotiations were broken off.

We answered that our intentions were good and had ever been so. He wrote again that he understood we were come to rob the Chinese and brought no money or merchandise for traffic, and entreated us to declare our meaning. Whereupon we answered him again that our intentions were good and the same as before we entreated to have traffic with them. He wrote again that if we persisted in our good intentions, we should send one of our Captains to him to confer with him about everything and make a treaty or truce with each other, for a number of years or for ever. We besought the aforesaid Totok that it might please him to permit us to come with a sloop before Amoy to be near at hand, for this business could be handled better from nearby than from a distance. This licence was granted to us at once, to come before Amoy with one or two ships. We then at last the 13th agreed together that our Commander Christiaen Fransz. with the sloops *Muyden* and *Erasmus* should sail to Amoy.

The 14th the sloops departed and came next day to Amoy, and we with the two ships continued to lie under the island.

Between the 17th and 18th, in the latter part of the night, I went with the boat to our sloops to get tidings how the matter stood, for it began to grieve us it lasted so long, which seemed on their setting out so nearby. But being on the way and near the sloops, we saw that one was on fire and the other had also three fire-junks alongside and stood in great peril by a great multitude of vessels, sampans and some war-junks, and we saw about fifty fire-junks. We went to the sloop *Erasmus*, which had valiantly put out one fire-junk, and got the other two out of her way, so that she was miraculously freed from the peril. But the sloop *Muyden's* foresail and fore-top-sail had caught fire, and she appeared to be beyond help ; she was burnt and soon blew up with men and all, being a most pitiful business. We went instantly to our ships with the sloop *Erasmus*.

Our men on the *Erasmus* related to us how the affair had befallen so far. They said : As soon as they were come before Amoy, there came at once a deputation on board to request that some of the chief persons should come on land to the Totok to speak together by word of mouth ; which the Commander did with courtesy refuse, saying he had no suitable interpreters therefor. But if the Totok pleased he would send some of his men with full power to conclude a treaty with them Upon that they returned to land.

Being come again they said : That the Totok had fully authorised them to that end and that all they should conclude with us would be firmly and indissolubly recognised and maintained by him. They then entered into negotiation and agreed and concluded that they would come and traffic with us at Tayowan and there bring us so much silk-goods as our capital would be good for; that they would not sail to the Manillas, Cambodia, Siam, Patany, Jambi, Andrigerry or other places without a pass from us; and they should also send four or six junks to Batavia to confer with our General regarding the Pescadores, from where they would be glad to have us move.

This treaty having been solemnly agreed to, they returned on land; and afterwards came again on board and begged us that some of our Captains would come on land to the Totok; that the treaty should be written and sworn on the one side in Chinese and the other side in Dutch so that the Totok could write to the Combon of Hockchu that this had been done in his presence. They brought with them three Mandarins as hostages, and (according to their custom) three arrows as a pledge.

Commander Christiaen Fransz, with the Council from the sloops, thereupon agreed that the Commander himself with Doede Florisz. Craegh, Captain of the *Muyden*, and Willem van Houdaen, Chief-Merchant on the *Erasmus*, should go on land to carry out the above-mentioned. Being come on land with about thirty men, among them the Captain of the *Erasmus*,

Jan Pietersz. Reus, they were (so it seemed) very well received. Tables were set out on the shore for the sailors, and the meal quickly served. The Commander instructed Jan Pietersz. Reus to have care of the men to take them presently on board again, while he, with the other delegates, was conducted to the house of the Totok. It appeared they designed to make the sailors drunken ; the Mandarins served the table, they desired Captain Jan Pietersz. Reus should also go up to the Totok. He did as if he were going to follow, but seeing (as he surmised) it was no fair dealing, bade the men stand up and fall into the boat and so with it to the ship.

In the evening (so it as was agreed) the steersman, Moses Claesz. of the sloop *Muyden*, went with a boat manned to the shore to fetch our three aforesaid Councillors. Coming on land they were taken and held by the Chinese. The men in the sloops knew not what to think wherefore the boat with our Councillors remained so long on land ; inquired of the hostages why they returned not : they answered : "They are merry". But it was but a poor merriment, for that same night about four hours before daybreak, they came (as related) with some fifty fire-junks to destroy the sloops and they did destroy the one, as related. The Chinese had also sent some Chinese beer to the sloops wherein they put poison to poison our men, but it was found out without doing injury; it seemed God willed it not.

These tidings grieved us all sorely, for it was a great loss to us and a godless piece of villainy by the Chinese; which God shall judge in His own time.

> What thing more evil in the world can be
> Than seeming friend who proves an enemy?

The 18th we fetched some firewood from the houses on the island of the Pagodas where we lay, then resolved to sail to the north side of the river being more safe anchorage from the fire-junks, for we now saw plainly, it was not friendship but enmity they sought with us.

The 19th the ship *Engelsche Beer* came from Japan to us; we related to them all our adventures and for this with other reasons the Council of the ships did assemble in the ship *Beer* and concluded what may be understood in this following resolution:

Resolution, taken by the chiefs of the ships lying before the river of Chinchu on the 24th November, 1623:

Whereas, setting forth from Japan on the 11th November it was thought meet, for the better security of our voyage to the Pescadores, for us to touch at the coast of China; therefore, God be praised, we came on the 19th before the river of Chinchu and found there the ships *Groningen*, *Samson* and *Erasmus*, from whom to our great sorrow we learned the distressful burning of the sloop *Muyden* as also the taking prisoner of the Commander Christiaen Fransz. with the other deputies who had on our part gone to treat with the Chinese for peace. And as the instructions of Commander Cornelis Reyersz. require that, whether there be war or peace, the river of Chinchu shall be held by ships; it appears that our comrades of the above-mentioned ships do complain sorely of being overburdened with sick men, in particular the *Samson*, having scarce men in health enough to weigh their anchor; who therefore would be forced to leave the coast or put over their sick on some other vessel to bring them to the Pescadores.

Therefore we have approved and resolved (hearing from the above-mentioned friends that the Commander Cornelis Reyersz. is departed from the Pescadores with most of the sick men to Taiwan, so that few sick remain in the Pescadores) to give of the victuals we have for the fleet to the above-named three ships: Ten thousand large apples, ten thousand mikans, twenty pigs, two hundred melons, and three oxen, so that the river of Chinchu shall not, to the damage of the Company, remain unguarded for want of refreshing.

And seeing also that by the captivity of Commander Christiaen Fransz. the fleet is deprived of its head, the Council doth hereby provisionally, till further order of the Commander Cornelis Reyersz, place and appoint Willem Ysbrantsz. Bontekoe, in all matters which may arise, to call together the council, preside thereover and as before to carry our flag on the mainmast etc.

Thus given and attested on the ship *Engelsche Beer*, date and year as above. Signed by

Isaac ven de Wercken
Frans Leendersz. Valk
Herman de Coningh
Pieter Fransz.
Jan Pietersz. Reus

These victuals did hearten our sick in great measure, we held the river so far as possible close and guarded; according to our orders, so that the Chinese could not go out free to the Manillas and other places; we took several of their junks and other vessels.

At last I sailed again to the Pescadores and my time being expired and having no mind to bind myself anew, although Mr Cornelis Reyersz. did strongly urge me thereto, offering me many good and better conditions than I had before, besides notable increase of salary; I obtained at last after much solicitation that I should go on another ship which lay ready to depart for Batavia, named *de Goede Hope*. The Commander Cornelis Reyersz. gave us an ample instruction, by which to regulate our ships on the voyage and in encounters with others, among which this short instruction:

JOURNAL OF

Instruction

for the persons of the Council of the ship *de Goede Hope* sailing from Pehu to Batavia.

Whereas it is the desire of our Masters[1] and of the Governor-General, that on all ships authority be given to some person in such affairs as may arise, to call together the council and to preside over the same.

Therefore, to this purpose we have approved to appoint Willem Ysbrantsz. Bontekoe, captain of the said vessel, who in all matters that may occur in the service of the Company, shall summon the council, preside over the same and have the first voice.

Jan de Moor, Merchant
Jan de Nayer, Mate
Chief Boatswain.
Second Mate—the fifth voice.

These above-mentioned persons of the council are strictly enjoined to accomplish the voyage, and also to further the service of the Company with all due diligence and obedience to the ample instructions given in the resolution dated 19th February, anno 1624.

Given in the Fort at the Pescadores this day 20th February, 1624.

Cornelis Reyersz.

The 21st Febuary I set sail with the ship *de Goede Hope* from the Pescadores to Batavia, but with instruction first to cross over to the coast of China, which we did ; but met with a great storm on coming near the coast and found our ship to be so slow to turn that we could scarce put her about with the foresail before the wind. She also did so leak that we must continually stand to the pumps ; found it therefore inadvisable to stay there longer, but decided to continue our voyage to Batavia. Held off before the wind ; 24th and 25th of the same month we passed the islands of Macao, with very variable weather.

The 6th March we came by *de Engelsche Beer*, whereof the Merchant was Isaac van de Wercken and Captain Frans Leendertsz. of Rotterdam. Came on board of us ; they related they had taken some hundred and sixty Chinese (men, women and children), whom we, following our instructions given us, would take over from them and charged them to stand by, but they declared their ship to be so unseaworthy and leaky that they could scarce hold it above water, and therefore were forced to keep their course to Batavia.

The 8th the Captain of *de Beer* brought two small beasts for our refreshing.

The 9th we went aboard *de Beer*, received again two beasts, a portion of beans, some pots of oil and other goods.

The 17th we came to anchor under Polepon, here fetched water and took over sixty-four Chinese from *de Beer*. Went also to cut wood.

The 20th we again set sail.

Between 25th and 26th same *de Beer* was driven away from us.

The 30th we came to anchor under the Man-eaters' island.

The 1st of April we weighed anchor and came next day, being the 2nd April, in the roadstead before Batavia.

I then once more made some journeys for stone to the above-mentioned islands between Bantam and Batavia.

I was now resolved at the first opportunity to go to Holland, finding the truth of the proverb the which is proved by experience : every bird returns gladly to the place where he was nested ; for whatever splendid countries, coasts and kingdoms a man may sail to and look over ; whatever conditions, profit or pleasures he may enjoy, would be but poor entertainment were we not supported by the hope of once upon a time relating our adventures at home ; for in that very hope do we call our journeyings " travels ", otherwise such hopeless wanderings would be no better to a man than exile.

While I was busied here in carrying stone to and from Batavia (as related) there were three ships to wit : the ship *Hollandia*, *Gouda*, and the ship *Middelburgh* being made ready to return to Patria—which opportunity I laid hold of : I made request to the Governor-General

Carpentier and his Council that I might depart therewith, the which was granted. They put me as captain on the ship *Hollandia*, being a most finely-equipped vessel. Commander Cornelis Reyersz. was meantime come from the Pescadores to Batavia with intent to return home, he was made Commander of the three above-mentioned ships; we had him on our ship; he was a dexterous man of much experience, who had done great service to the Company in many things.

Here in Batavia I had speech with my fellow townsman, Willem Cornelis Schouten, he came on the ship *Middelburgh* to return home in company with us.[1]

The 6th February, 1625, we three above-mentioned ships did set sail from Batavia to return home, so it were God's will.

Touched in passing at Bantam where several of our ships lay; from them we took a great rope and a foresail, took leave of our friends with a westerly wind, which for us was against the wind. We therefore tacked till under the island Sibesi, that lies on the inside of the Strait of Sunda, next to Sumatra. We lay there for three or four days waiting for a favourable wind, also because the current ran so strong into the Strait.

The 15th, we set sail with the land wind, made a tack and the 16th got outside the Strait of Sunda, having the wind westerly. Coursed to the south, with feeble breezes, but the wind freshened from day to day; continued southwards, hoped to get a southerly wind.

The 27th we had the wind from southwards; were at the height of 17 degrees south latitude. Veered then to westward and set our course westerly to the Cape Bon Esperance, till we came to the height of 19 degrees south latitude. We had then S.E. wind which became more easterly as we went; we held westerly with a strong breeze, carrying as much sail as we could.

The 15th March, in the morning having shot the sun in its rising, we found 22 degrees, the north-west shifting of the compass diminishing. This same day our Commander Cornelis Reyersz. became very sick.

The 16th, 17th and 18th it began so fiercely to blow that sailing under a tight-reefed foresail and the spritsail we could not hold our course within eight points of the compass; we feared that in the night we might drift away from one another. And as we carried the signal light, I went to the Commander in the cabin and there called together the ship's council. I said to the Commander, who (as related) lay very sick: "Should we thus continue to sail to-night, I fear by morning we shall have lost one another, for our men cannot keep the ship within eight points. I judge it is best to take in our sails by daylight and let the ship lie at hull, and when our companions see that they will do the same; I trust we shall not this night be scattered so wide but we shall to-morrow be in sight of each other". Thereupon answered the Commander: " If that seems good to you, captain, let us then do so ". The which we did. Took in by day our foresail and the sprit-sail, made them faſt to the yard, and lay at hull.

Our two consorts, to wit, the ship *Gouda* and *Middelburgh*, perceiving that, did likewise: took in their sails and lay at hull as we did. Veered with our bow over to southward. At six glasses of the night the wind began to blow so terrifically hard that to him who has never heard or seen the like it would appear impossible for the wind to have such force. The wind was at all points of the compass, for the compass turned round continually so that we could not see how our course lay. The ship by the force of the wind sank so low into the water, as it were the wind came on her ſtraight from above, and it seemed that the anchors which hung on the bow came to the water; indeed, we thought the ship was about to sink. At laſt our mainmaſt was blown overboard and broke about three fathoms above the deck, by which the ship then rose again. We stood together with our heads touching, yet could not shout or speak that we could hear one another, that is those who were on deck.

This tempestuous strong wind, which is called a hurricane, continued for about six or eight glasses, then the wind began to lessen. While it blew most fiercely, the sea was smooth as a table because it could not raise itself; but when the wind lessened, the sea rose so mightily that it seemed the ship would turn turtle. The rolling at last sprang a plank under water, whereby we shipped so much water from above, that we were greatly hindered, for the water ran into the hold so that we had seven feet of water in the ship before we knew what had happened; at which we feared the ship was about to sink. Pumped with all our pumps, but the water seemed to be rising in spite of it. At this we were overwhelmed, for it was a hopeless chance. Then the pumps became useless so we could not pump; for the bottom part of the hold was filled with pepper which stopped up the pumps. We had sixty pieces of ordnance both brass and iron that lay in the hold under the pepper which was stored on a platform halfway up the hold; by the rolling of the ship these became loose and with their ears broke through the platform, so that the pepper fell through into the hold, and as the bottom flooring of the hold was forced up by the water, the pepper was all washed into the space underneath it into which the pumps open. Yet as we hoped and trusted that the ship was still whole at the bottom, we did our best to do all we

PLATE IX

" The hurricane continued for about six or eight glasses."

[face p. 132

could ; drew out the pumps and wound pieces of old flags round them at the ends and set those same ends down on the bottom flooring, instead of through it, each in a basket. Then fell again to pumping with all our might ; and now the pumps remained clear. We saw immediately that the water lessened, at which we again took courage.

Our blown off mainmast lay clanking the whole night under the bottom and on the side of the ship so that we feared it might make our bottom leak. The men in the hold called out : " Cut away everything that holds it fast and let it drift ! " We did what we could, we hacked the standing rigging through to windward but on the leeside, as the ship rolled and swung so mightily, we could not get a foothold ; we had to leave it so for the night, but in the day we cut off all we could see and so made ourselves free of the driftage.

In the morning we looked round for our two consorts but missed one of them, to wit the ship *Gouda*, but the ship *Middelburgh* lay to windward of us. She had lost all her masts, with bowsprit, gallion and all, save her mizzenmast. So we were both in a bad way. What was to be done ! The ship *Gouda* did not come into sight, we feared she was sunk ; and so she was, as we believe, for during the night we drifted through a place where the water was very brown and smoother than in other parts ; one or two of the men drew some up with a bucket, they said it was pepper ; already then a fear did smite us that all was not well with one or both of our consorts. Although ourselves in no very good case, this loss of the ship *Gouda* did sorely grieve our hearts.

The next day the weather became fair. The ship *Middelburgh* lay (as said) to windward of us, but we could not come near to one another ; we lay both as it were impotent. Before daylight the *Middelburgh* put out the yawl and rowed to us, came at daybreak behind our ship under the gallery and called out to us, at which we were marvellously startled for we never expected anybody to be near about us. We looked from the gallery and heard it was the yawl from the *Middelburgh*, dropped the man-rope out behind, by which the captain, whose name was Jan Dijcke, of Flushing, came over to us with one other. They related their adventures and how they were situated, and we ours likewise to them. In a woeful tone they said to us that they had lost all their masts and rigging, and if we could not help them they would never be able to make land. We had kept our foremast and bowsprit with the mizzen mast, as also our mainyard ; that was because I had our yards hauled down before the wind rose and they had kept their yards up ; and had thereby lost their whole rigging. We had to make the best of a bad job. We therefore resolved to give the *Middelburgh* our mainyard with our foretop maſt, and a spar of forty palms which we had in the ship. They made sure that so they could put up ſtumps sufficient to make land. It was also agreed, that when we gave them this, each should do his beſt to get the first land he could; we set our minds on the Bay of Sancta Lucia in the island of Madagascar.

This was thus resolved by the full council in the cabin, and as I was captain, it was for me to give these orders to the men. When I came on deck to command, the men rose againſt me and ſtrongly objected to it, saying: "We are in a worse plight than the *Middelburgh*, we will not give it to them". There I ſtood and looked at them. But I spoke with soft words: "Men, think what you do, for should we leave the *Middelburgh* here helpless, it is certain she cannot help herself and will be wrecked, for they can make no sail. We are Chriſtian folk, then let us show ourselves Chriſtians. Think what we should desire were we in their place and let us do the same to our fellow-men". I gave them as many good words as I could put together.

At laſt they gathered together, began to put their heads together and said one to the other: "What shall we do? We are all even so, Chriſtian men, as the Captain says, and if the *Middelburgh* were loſt, what should we have to say?" Whereupon they came again to me at the mainmast and said: "Well, Captain when we have fitted the *Middelburgh* with these things, may we then part company with her?" To which I answered: Yes, that it was so resolved in the cabin. At that they let it go: took down the foretop mast and smacked it overboard with the mainyard and the fourteen palm spar. Then the two from the *Middelburgh* took leave of us and rowed to their ship with the stuff behind them, we should find each other again in the Bay Sancta Lucia if God willed it. Then our men asked again: "May we now part company with them?" I said: "Yes". Our foreyard lay on deck, I said: "Lay hold of the gear of the foreyard and hoist up the foreyard". Which they did immediately and ran the foreyard up right to the sheave-hole. Before that it had always seemed almost impossible to hoist the foreyard, but willing hands made short work.

The 22nd we departed from the *Middelburgh*; we set our course for Madagascar, which was nearest to us, and had sight of land on the 30th.. We sailed close under the land; saw where the sea broke on some shallows, that were unknown to us. We were to our reckoning eight or nine miles eastwards of the Bay of Sancta Lucia, feared to go far from the coast knowing we were so damaged, resolved therefore to cast anchor (it was about twenty-five fathom deep) to put out the sloop and row or sail along the coast as was suitable, to see if we could find the aforesaid Bay. Upon this I set off from the ship with the sloop well-manned. Found the aforementioned bay about eight or ten miles from where the ship lay ; sounded the islands and depths with the sounding-lead over and over again, and found it was a fitting place for the ship. Having done that we returned joyfully to the ship. Came the next day back on board and related all that had befallen us. Weighed our anchor and sailed thither ; brought the ship in with God's help, whereat we all rejoiced greatly and thanked God for His mercy.

The 1st April we determined to unload the ship and make tents on land to store the goods, and to clear the bottom apertures. And as I went with the boat to shore I saw that the sea ran fairly high, therefore I thought it not advisable to bring our lading on land, for there would be peril that both sloop and boat might be broken to pieces. For this reason we resolved to clear the hold, and keep the goods in the ship, which we did. We carried the lading from the forepart of the ship in sacks and filled up the constable's room on the upper deck, and hastily made the forepart of the ship quite empty. Put up a partition across the deck at the mainmast so that the goods could not shift towards us from aft ; took up the bottom flooring, cleared the bottom space and apertures ; put ropes from fore to midway the ship through the apertures to keep them clear if by chance they should again stop up. Then we stowed the lading out of the constable's room and upper deck forward again. Having done that we took out the lading from the back part of the ship and put it away in the constable's room and upper deck, and cleared the bottom space and the apertures in that part also. We then hauled the ropes through the apertures from the mast further to the stern part of the ship so that if needful we could pull the ropes backwards and forwards through the apertures. Meanwhile we had speech with the inhabitants. We shewed them that our mast and our rigging were much out of order and asked if there were means to get another mast. They could understand our meaning, and waved us to inland; they went with us and there shewed us suitable trees. Said they would help us in all we needed. I went there with men, ropes, tackle, axes and saws; procured what we wanted; dragged the timber and brought it with much difficulty near the ship. Set our carpenters to work; from the thick end of the timber that was about eighteen palm thick and twenty-eight foot long, we made a piece to fit on the stump of our broken mast; sawed a dovetail in the thickest end and cut our stump which, as related, was broken off 3½ fathom above the upper deck, to a sharp point, then set on the new piece fitting them together. We then put four fishplates thereon and wrapped that together

"We were busied every day to repair our damage."

[face p. 138

so that it was a strong taut piece of work. Then took our mizzen-top, sawed it through lengthwise and put the sides as far from each other as we would have the top, and filled the opening with planks till the top was a good one.

We were busied every day to repair our damage, in the ship as well as on land. We had some irons such as are used on the rope-yards to make rope-work. Set one up on land; cut one of our heavy cables in pieces, loosened them and made from them all our running rigging. We endeavoured thus to help ourselves as best we could.

The news that we were there spread far and wide in the land; thereupon came the inhabitants from far and near, drove their beasts to us and there encamped. Put up their tents and brought us everything they had; apples, lemons, citrons and milk, which they first part-boiled before selling it to us for it would not last, but was quickly sour. We trafficked with them and bought some of their beasts. Their fishers went out to sea and brought us their fish which we bought or bartered with them. These people were devoted to us; they shewed us they had enemies in that same country. Besought us by signs to help them and they would do all they could for us. Here was also wax and honey; they sold us a portion.

We understood from them that their king could

speak Spanish; he lived five or six days' journey from the coast. Sent two of our men to the king to ask if he would sell us some rice; one of them was named Abraham Stevensz, of Flushing, who spoke good Spanish, with another young man. They came to the King and were well received. Delivered their message and asked to buy some rice. But the king said they had that year been much plagued by locusts who had eaten up most of the rice; which I myself could well believe for I had seen (after walking some way inland) how the locusts rose up off the land as it were in a cloud moving towards me, and flew against my breast and body so thick that I could scarce get my breath. They had wings to fly and being on the ground they hopped after the manner of hopping fowls. The king said they could set as many as three or four hundred men to guard the rice and keep the locusts off it, yet it was of little help. Therefore they had no rice to give us. We saw that the inhabitants took the locust, pulled off the wings to roast them on the fire and did eat them. Signed us that we should do the same, but we had no stomach for it. The king came down with our two men to the ship; gave us four beasts, for the which we gave him two muskets. He then said to us also that he could spare no rice.

After we had lain here eleven days the Commander Cornelis Reyersz. died and went to rest in the Lord.

We buried him on an island (which lies in the entrance of the Bay), well wooded, beneath a fine green tree, the best we could find. He was a good man. To this death the following verses may be applied :

> Death follows us where'er we go,
> Not one of us escapes his fate.
> But when or where doth no man know
> If East or West or soon or late.
> He who accepts what God hath sent,
> Be't Life or Death, he is content.

Our musketeers shot three times over the grave and from the ship a salute of five shots was fired ; we then took our leave of the grave. Started to work again to finish our business with the ship. And as the men often wandered away to seek pleasure more than work, I, knowing the state we were in, admonished them every day with gentle words : "Men, let us do our best to get ready, so that we do not waste our time here, for we are victualled but for eight months and should we spend all our time here and eat up all our victuals, then we'll have to return to Batavia" ; and for that, I knew well, they had no mind. So I tried to give them a heart for the work, and instead of to command I was fain to implore, such as more often happens in a like case, for we still had much work to do. It was here with me as with Scipio Africanus, who (as I have heard) was wont to say: "I am never less idle than when I am idle, and never less alone than when I am alone" For I had in the night enough to do to invent and contrive how by day we should set about making and fitting all things, and so keep each man to his work and give contentment to all; so that in the end they were convinced in their mind, and every man did his best, until the 22nd April; then we were in order again and lay with our yards across, ready to continue our voyage. We brought our water-barrels full of water and our men got as many apples and lemons as each could put in his berth.

The inhabitants of this island were mostly black; some had hair that hung by their heads, others had it curled like sheep's wool. The women had their hair plaited in small plaits round their head, and they smeared it with oil till it shone in the sun; the men mostly did likewise. The greater number had no more than a small cloth round their loins to cover their shame and some went quite naked without shame.

The 23rd we determined to sail the next day at morning with the land-wind, but in that same night, two of our men who had the watch rowed to land with our small sloop and ran away to the blacks, so that we could not find them. At this we were much astonished for they had helped to make the whole ship ready and went away just the last night, and to such barbarous folk too, in whom I could see no knowledge of God or

His Commandments. One of these deserters was named Hilke Jopkis from Friesland and another Gerrit Harmesz, of Norden. We surmised they had too much traffic with the women, who with their seeming fair promises had drawn their hearts to stay with them, for women are mighty instruments to ensnare men, whereof the examples are unnecessary to recall. Think only of Samson, David, and Solomon. We saw here many children who were almost white, and whose fair coloured hair hung from their heads; we reckoned these to be begotten of Hollanders who had been in the Bay before us. The women were keen to have intercourse with our men, and had there been in this place wine or beer to be sold as well as there were women to be had, we had not so soon accomplished our work. But now when they had been with the women, they returned meek as lambs to their work. This I say of many, excepting the well-behaved.

By the deserting of these two men our sailing was delayed a day longer, for we went that day on land to seek them; had sight of them, but when they were aware of us they retreated from us and we must needs leave them there.

Then the 25th April we set sail with the land-wind; ran to the south with temperate weather till 10th May with a westerly wind; had change of wind and weather with rain; wind very tempestuous from

W.S.W. Veered then over to northward; found we had not enough press of sail aft to be able to tack into the wind, so we veered before the wind and kept close to the wind to sail to windward of the island of Madagascar. The weather every day increased in strength, with strong W.S.W. wind, that we were forced to take in our topsails and followed our course above Madagascar till we had sight of land the 28th May named Terra de Natal. Nearing land the weather became fair with clear sky, but the swell was very deep, huge billows coming on from the Cape Bonesperance. We then held off from the coast, observed that a strong current ran near the shore which drew us towards the Cape, it was a wonder to see how swift the land passed by us; this gave us hope to double the Cape easily.

In the night we again had intemperate weather with mist and rain, by which for three or four days we ran out from the coast with tight-reefed sails; we had the wind westerly with hollow billows from all points which caused the ship often to shift her limbs that it creaked. Had she not been a strong ship she could never have remained whole. When the weather became a little quieter, we veered again over to northward towards the coast; by reason of the tempestuous weather we could make no reckoning, but kept on our tack till we had sight of land, when it cleared up again. We then took our height and found it 35 degrees, by which we saw the land was Cape Agulhas which lies in the height of 35 degrees. Held out from the coaſt; W.S.W. with wind and rain; it began again to blow so hard and the contrary seas ran so high againſt one another and broke over the ship that it seemed the ship would be smothered therein, yet by God's mercy we wreſtled through, which had hardly seemed possible.

This continued four days; we lay now with one sail and then with two reefed foresails. Our ship was so ſtiff that we could not well hold her without a sail.

The 6th June the sea began to run calm and we had fair weather. Took our height; found 32 degrees and 16 minutes, by which we saw that we were above or inside the Cape of Bonesperance, for the Cape lies in 34½ degrees. It then became more and more such right fair weather that we did seem to be in Heaven, who had so late been in Hell. And while before we were so tormented and in truth hopeless to double the Cape, yet with the current we had pushed beyond it, againſt the wind and such tempeſtuous weather, to the wonder of us all; and as before we could carry none or scarce any sail, we could now put up always two topsails. Set our course for the island of Sancta Helena; had the wind S.E., and E.S.E., with a fair breeze.

The 14th June came in sight of the same, at which we did all rejoice. Ran close along the coaſt. On coming round the point, towards the Church valley where the watering-place is, we saw a Spanish carack lying right before the Church valley. As soon as they saw us they brought out an anchor to the landward, and shortened in close to the shore, and immediately with the boats carried some guns on land and made a battery. We with the ship *Hollandia*, coming near them, ran into a whirlwind, for the coast is very steep and the winds whirled over the land. Therefore we could not reach them for our intention was to board them, cut their ropes and pull them to sea. We could have done this, for she carried her guns so high that with our ship we could have lain under their shot. Had our intent succeeded, we doubted not to have mastered them; but by the said whirlwind we could not get closer than a musket shot to them.

We manned our yawl; sent the Junior-Merchant Herman de Coningh (he was from The Hague) with a peace-flag to them. Seeing that, they hastily manned their boat and came to meet our men in between the two ships. They hailed each other. Asked us from where we came. Our men answered from Java and that we had drifted from our consort and awaited her every hour. Our men asked where they came from, they said from Goa. They asked further (seeing they occupied the watering-place) if they would permit us to come and fetch water, which we had much need of, and having that we should immediately depart. Upon which they shouted: "Anda pero, Anda canaly", with many more abusive words. Then our men returned with the sloop to our ship and related to us what had happened.

Thereupon we at once called the ship's council together to consider what we should do. Resolved that the yawl should at once return and ask if they had determined whether we should come to fetch water or not, and if as before they would not consent thereto, then our men should return to the ship, and we give them so much time to consider as the length of one glass, and if ere it was run out they came and agreed to our request, then we would leave them in peace, and if not we should immediately fire away at them. With this resolution the yawl rowed again to them with the peace-flag. They came again with their boat to meet our men. In their boat stood a monk with a hood on his head, who hailed our men. Our Junior-Merchant De Coningh having said his speech was given a refusal as before: "Anda pero, anda canaly! We do not want to see you here, begone!" Our men coming on board reported this to us. We then let the bell be rung, said our prayers, set a glass of half an hour in the socket and as soon as that same glass had run out and we saw no sign of their coming, we fired at them quickly with demi-cannons, of which we had eleven, and shot into the carack so that she shook, for she was easy to hit; their foreship or castle was, so seemed, as high as our fore-top, although we had a ship of 1,000 tons. We continued to shoot at them till they shot little more from the carack, but with the pieces which they had brought on land from the carack and set up on their battery, they shot steadily at our ship and hit her as if they had laid it in by hand. For each shot was one that touched us, two, three, four foot above the water, so that we feared they would sink us; we had several wounded. Among them our second carpenter by name Bokjen, of Dort, had both legs shot off; lived a little time, but died suddenly, by reason of which we could not remain lying there. Resolved to bring out an anchor on the shore-side where a reef lay. We shortened in behind this reef till we were free of their shots from the battery.

We lay so near the coast that one could have thrown a stone on to the land. Then came the night. We summoned all the officers to the cabin, with the steward; inquired of him how much water we still had, and reckoned over how much we required, knowing we had yet to pass the Æquinoctial Line, and then it might still be a long time ere we came to Holland. We found accordingly that we could give no more than four mugs a day of water. So we asked the officers, and the officers spoke with the men what they thought—

whether they would engage in a life and death fight to have water against the enemy who held the watering-place, or should we continue our voyage home and be content with four mugs of water a day. This question therefore being put to all, it was agreed unanimously by all the officers and the whole ship's crew to continue our voyage and be content with four cups of water a day. Immediately weighed anchor to set sail.

But when it was day, as we were beginning to tow the ship out from the land, the Specks came up on the coast with musket and shot from above down into the ship and at the boat, so that it was scarce to be stood; yet (by God's help) we got off the shore. Had we stayed there another hour, we should have been in great peril to lose many of our company.

This aforesaid carack while lying there was sunk (as was afterwards told me) by reason of our having so hit her. For, some while later there came six Dutch ships to refresh themselves, they saw her lying on the bottom, and the Portuguese had taken her lading, as much as they could, and put it on land, as well as her ordnance which they had put on a battery they had thrown up. From there they shot so lustily at these six ships that they could not come to land; and must therefore, even as we, depart without refreshing.

We set our course to N.W., to the island Ascension, with a good wind and quick progress; yet we had no sight of it. We saw only, when we reckoned to be thereabouts, a great multitude of sea-fowl. The wind began to increase as much as we could bear, with which stiff wind we passed the Æquinoctial Line without hindrance; while on our voyage outwards we were held six weeks ere we could pass it, mostly by calms and then again sudden squalls by which it seemed that all we had on would be blown to pieces.

The 12th September, when we were three days less than three months from St. Helena, we came in the height of 34 degrees 34 minutes north of the Æquinoctial Line. We here had better weather, then drifted in a calm; set to work in the morning after breaking fast, clewed up our sails, scraped and scrubbed our ship on the outside, for it was all grown very rough and foul; we hoped thereby to make better sailing.

The 13th it was fair weather with a light breeze from E.S.E., went north-east by north.

The 15th, S.S.W. wind, the course as before; took our height in the afternoon and found 28 degrees north latitude. Tore off our fore-sail and put up another.

The 16th we also changed our fore-top sail, saw much rock-weed drifting; course as before with a continual fair S.W. wind.

The 17th we found our height to be 30 degrees 48 minutes; now changed our maintop sail; with variable winds. In the night the wind came north-east and east, with thunder and lightning; took in our top sails.

The 18th hoisted our topsails again with our sprit-sail; the course N.E. It was misty, sometimes with rain; could not take our height.

The 19th it began to blow so hard from the S.S.W. and S.W. that we took in our topsails and our sprit-sail was blown away. Our main-sail that we endeavoured to haul in was torn in pieces. That night we held on with the fore-sail; towards day the wind abated; we again hoisted our topsails.

The 20th put up another main-sail and a sprit-sail, took our height and found 35 degrees 13 minutes north latitude.

The 24th was dark clouds with gusts of rain; took off our top-gallant mast.

The 26th we had the height of 43 degrees 12 minutes.

The 27th the wind S.W., the course N.E. by N. In the forenoon there came a dove flying on to our ship, but the men being so desirous to catch it, it flew up again and fell down in the water. Took our height and found 44 degrees 53 minutes.

The 1st October the weather was fair, the wind E.S.E., the course straight across the wind, N.E. by N. Afternoon we took the height of 48 degrees 30 minutes, which is the height of Ushant.

The 2nd day, in the morning, saw a sail north-west of us about three miles; clewed up our sails and waited for her. Late in the afternoon she came near us, we spoke to her; it was an Englishman from near Plymouth, came from Newfoundland. We bought from them two thousand fish; fetched the Captain on board of us, by name Mr Smallwater. Went E. and E. by south; weather became misty with rain.

The 4th, the Englishman came again on board of us; we entertained him with the best we had; our height was 49 degrees 46 minutes.

The 5th began to blow hard, our fore-sail was blown to pieces. The Englishman now drifted away from us. The wind was S.S.W.

The 6th day saw two sails, one at the side of us, one behind. Held to S.E., to sail the Channel. Our height was 50 degrees 20 minutes.

The 7th the weather was fair, wind south, course E.S.E., we saw no ships. Put up another sail again.

The 8th we were in the height of 49 degrees 42 minutes, wind as before, but soon ran west. Set our course S.E. by E., cast our head as we had done some days previous, but could get no ground. Towards evening died Captain Stryker, who had been captain over the soldiers; he was a valiant and worthy man, well-exercised in the art of war; he was from the Rhineland, from Wesel or thereabout.

The 10th day at evening, we threw our lead and found ground about seventy fathom.

The 11th in the morning we again found ground at seventy fathom, and evening at 60 fathom with grey sand. Our height was 49 degrees and 55 minutes, the wind south; set our course E. by N. and N.E.

The 12th, sounded on fifty fathom and continued to cast the lead every four glasses. Found generally fifty, fifty-two, fifty-three fathom, and at night we found fifty-six to sixty fathom and grey, white and sometimes some black sand. Saw also a ship coming towards us ahead, but it grew so misty we lost sight thereof.

The next day the wind was east with cloudy misty weather and calm. Two or three days later we had sight of land, which we found to be Ireland. Ran into Kinsale. There lay there an English King's ship with two tiers of cannon, and seeing I had knowledge that the Dutch Company, our Lords and Masters, were in no good friendship with the English[1], I was doubtful to let the men go in too large numbers on land, fearing to have trouble with this King's ship. I therefore cast anchor to seawards of her, thinking: "Should she make trouble, we can get away to sea, and should she follow us then we shall have no need to worry". I went on board her, invited the Commander in our ship; he came. I asked him of all events, among other things if he had any orders to harm us in any way. He answered "No", and was friendly and of good cheer with us. Yet I was not assured; had a feaſt made ready on shore, invited him thereto and we drank to one another; and in the merry-making of the meal I asked again if he had no orders to moleſt us. Once more he answered "No", and related that while we lay there he had written to England but received no orders to that intent; yet I dared not put much truſt therein.

Meanwhile there came to us two Convoys, who had been cruising to find us, having had knowledge that we lay there. Of the one was captain Jacob Jansz, of Edam, and of the other Pieter Gijsen, of Rotterdam. Thus was our back better protected if it came to the worſt.

While thus lying here our men ran so much on shore that I saw little chance of getting them to the ship again. I warned them, whenever I fell in with some of them that they should return to the ship for we ought now to continue our voyage; it was already autumn, the winter was at hand, and we had a foul, unwieldy ship. I did show them the peril there was to bring to land so heavy a ship so late in the year; yet it helped but little, the men ſtayed on land, it looked as if they were home already, they ate and drank with a will.

I went at laſt to the Mayor of the town, asked him if there were no means of bringing our men on board. He said no, he knew of none; but when I had spoken with his wife and presented her with a piece of fine linen, then he said, when I asked him again, that he would soon help me. He immediately caused some drummers to go through the town and call out everywhere that all men be warned, whosoever should give credit for more than seven shillings to any of the Hollanders from the East Indiaman, he would lose his money. On this proclamation, most of them (as their reckoning was already beyond this sum) were thrust out of doors; they came then to me. I wanted to have them at once on board, but they would rather remain a little longer.

Thereupon I caused the anchors to be weighed, the sails unfurled and began to sail out of the bay. Then they fell into sloops and other craft like ants and came on board. The innkeepers and alehouse wives also came on board and demanded their money, the which I gave them and put the sum against each man's reckoning in the book. Now we had all our men again with us, save three or four who had promised themselves to women whom they afterwards married; these we let stay there. We sailed from there with the convoys and came with reasonable speed the 16th November to Zeelandt. The Lord be praised and thanked, Who hath thus far helped me through so many perils, I having been away in all about one month less than seven years.

Hereby I did intend to bring an end to my writing, seeing that my voyage was accomplished. But as I before related, the ship *Middelburgh* the 22nd March did part from us very damaged, with intent to find each other in the Bay of St. Lucia, where we arrived the 31st, and departed therefrom the 25th April, without in that time nor during our whole return voyage having seen or heard of her, nor afterwards ever did she come to safety; so must I (though it doth not of necessity belong to my voyages, and yet is not so far removed fom them that the Reader should blame me for enlarging my history with anything strange and unsuitable) inform the said Reader what since the time of our parting has befallen her, according to the most certain tidings and most credible presumption.[1] I the more willingly undertake this task since thereby I shall have cause to relate to posterity the end of our all-famous fellow-citizen of Hoorn, Willem Cornelisz Schouten, my particular friend, which has not reached the ears everyone, for he (as aforesaid) had sailed on the ship *Middelburgh*. The matter is as follows: While we lay in the Bay of St. Lucia, we heard from the inhabitants that a ship was lying in the Bay of Antongil, but we knew not for certain if this were the *Middelburgh* or not. On going away from there, we hoped to find her in St. Helena or to wait for her there, but by reason of the Spanish carak (as related) we could not come in to that island and so continued our voyage. Some time later Captain Pieter Gerritsz, *Bier-en-Broodtpot*, of Hoorn, came from the East Indies to the Cape Bonesperance and there found letters which the ship *Middelburgh*, had left there according to custom, wherein was related that they had intended to go into the Bay of St. Lucia, as was agreed between us, but had run so far below it that they came into the Bay of Antongil and there fitted themselves out with all they were in need of, and also that there some of their company had died, among them also the above-mentioned Willem Cornelisz Schouten, whom they there buried.

Upon whose death the following verses were composed:

In this our western world, where he was born and bred,
Brave Schouten could not rest; his inmost soul afire
Urged him to seek beyond, to voyage and strive ahead.
'Tis meet then that he lies i' the world of his desire,
Safe after all his travels. Oh great and eager mind,
Repose in blessed peace! Yet if thy soul refuse
In narrow Antongil for e'er to stay confined,
Then (as in earthly life so fearless thou didst choose
The unknown channel 'twixt the seas of East and West,
Outstripping the sun's course by a whole day and night),
Ascend thou up, this time surpassing the sun's height,
And find in heaven with God hope and eternal rest.

This was the end of this worthy man. These letters further related their adventures, in particular how they vere situated in coming to that place, while lying there, and how and when they departed therefrom. From that time forth no tidings came from them direct, so that here would have been the end thereof but from the Portuguese and from Portugal is later news come to hand, to wit: How that the aforesaid ship *Middelburgh* coming to the island of St. Helena was surrounded by two caracks, against which she put up a brave fight, and shot at least one carack afire. Seeing which, the other came to help her consort to put out the fire which they, so it is related, did quench; but as the Portuguese by this skirmishing feared to be removed from the island, and as the night was at hand, they drifted apart and let the *Middelburgh* go.

Such are the last tidings received of this ship; it is likely that she was lost on her way, and maybe in this fight with the caracks, had already received so much as made her sink. It might also be surmised that she was lost through want of victuals and refreshing, but seeing that she had been to the Cape and there refreshed, can scarce believe such to be the case. Be it as it may, it is ever a most woeful business that they did not come to safety, and moveth me to eternal gratitude that God so graciously hath saved and preserved me, that is with the ship *Hollandia*, from such apparent perils. I pray that His goodness may continue with me from now and ever more, Amen.

FINIS

NOTES

INTRODUCTION

[1] *Page* 12. See e.g. W. P. Groeneveldt, *De Nederlanders in China* (Vol. XLVIII of the *Bijdragen uitgegeven door het Kon. Instituut voor de Taal-, Land- en Volkenkunde van Nederl. Indië*, 1898), p. 322.

[2] *Page* 12. *Ib.*, p. 89.

[3] *Page* 12. See p. 153.

[1] *Page* 14. Groeneveldt, *op. cit.*, p. 189.

[1] *Page* 16. It is possible to obtain a complete view of the enterprise from Groeneveldt's *De Nederlanders in China*. This work, which was never continued beyond the year 1624, contains Reyertsz's own official journal and extracts from his and Nieuwenroode's correspondence with Batavia.

[1] *Page* 17. Groeneveldt, *op. cit.*, p. 131.

TEXT

[1] *Page* 23. Two of the Cape Verde Islands. They were in the possession not of the Spaniards, but of the Portuguese, between whom Bontekoe never makes a clear distinction; and in fact Portugal, from the conquest in 1580 to the rising in 1640, formed part of the Spanish Empire.

[1] *Page* 25. An island group off the coast of Brazil. Ships had to follow a course so far West in order to get the full advantage of the current in the Southern Atlantic.

[1] *Page* 28. The island of Mauritius had been taken by the Dutch from the Portuguese as early as 1598 and had been called after Prince Maurice, the Stadtholder. It served as a station on the way to Java, but was abandoned when, in 1651, the Cape had been occupied for the same purpose. The island of Mascarenhas is now called Réunion.

[1] *Page* 31. It was a common practice to leave messages of this kind in any of the possible stopping places on the way to the Indies, on

boards or stones. Several stones with inscriptions dating from before the occupation in 1651 have been found at the Cape and are preserved in the Museum at Capetown.

[1] *Page* 37. The Strait of Sunda is actually between 6 and 6½ degrees, southern latitude.

[1] *Page* 43. That is to say from Schleswig. Germans from Westphalia and from the coastal districts were numerous in the Dutch mercantile marine and in the service of the Dutch East India Company.

[1] *Page* 54. It was probably the island of Engano.

[1] *Page* 59. See the Introduction, p. 10. "General" is commonly used instead of the full title "Governor-General".

[1] *Page* 69. Which of the numerous islands in the Strait of Sunda these three islands were it is difficult to say. Possibly the Krakatoa group.

[1] *Page* 71. Willem Cornelisz Schouten of Hoorn was ship's master on Jacques le Maire's voyage round the world (1615-17). In the published journal of that expedition his conduct was unduly praised at the expense of that of Le Maire. In reality Schouten seems to have behaved very badly.

[2] *Page* 71. A Spanish or Portuguese vessel, with a high "castle" aft.

[1] *Page* 72. "Right-in-the-Way."

[2] *Page* 72. Having passed St. Nicholas Point.

[3] *Page* 72. See Introduction.

[4] *Page* 72. Frederik Houtman, brother of Cornelis Houtman, the leader of the first Dutch expedition to the Indies (1595). Frederik, who had sailed with his brother, had in 1605 been made the first governor of Amboina. He was a man of parts, an astronomer and editor of a Malay dictionary. The former capacity helps to explain his possession of a telescope, at this time still an exceedingly rare instrument.

[1] *Page* 73. "The Maiden of Dordrecht."

[2] *Page* 73. Bontekoe omits the dates in this part of his story, but he probably arrived at Batavia before the end of the year 1619. It was only on May 30th of the same year that Coen had taken and

burned down the native town of Jacatra, to found the central seat of Dutch power in the East on its ruins. See the Introduction.

[1] *Page* 74. *Boot*—boat.

[1] *Page* 75. Ternate is one of the Molucca islands. The fortresses in the Moluccas were the first erected anywhere by the Dutch Company.

[1] *Page* 75. Gresse or Griesk, not far from Soerabaja; the Dutch factory there served largely for the purchase of rice and other provisions needed for the garrisons in the Moluccas.

[2] *Page* 75. Solor is a small island East of Flores. The fortress was called Henricus.

[1] *Page* 76. Larantoeka is a place on the East coast of Flores.

[2] *Page* 76. *Specks*, a nickname by which Bontekoe indiscriminately indicates Spaniards or Portuguese. *Speck* in Dutch means bacon.

[3] *Page* 76. Corracorras, a kind of native vessel.

[4] *Page* 76. Blau: Ambelau.

[5] *Page* 76. The inlet is on the North side of the island of Amboina. Combello is the point of a peninsula of the island of Ceram. The spices were, of course, what took the Dutch to the Moluccas.

[1] *Page* 77. Here meaning the place where the fortress of Victoria stood, in the district of Amboina called Leitimor.

[2] *Page* 77. Maleyen: not identified.

[3] *Page* 77. Herman van Speult was the man who, a few years later, in 1623, ordered the execution of the English factors, who were convicted, under torture, of conspiracy against Dutch authority, the affair known as "the Amboyna massacre".

[4] *Page* 77. A small Molucca island, west of Malmalieua.

[5] *Page* 77. Boeton, an island to the S.E. of Celebes.

[1] *Page* 78. Little Java: Madoera.

[2] *Page* 78. The Thousand Islands.

[1] *Page* 79. The Porpoise.

[1] *Page* 80. Macao was a Portuguese stronghold. See Introduction.

[2] *Page* 80. The Manillas: The Philippines.

[3] *Page* 80. Balimbam: Palembang, now called Banka Strait.

[1] *Page* 81. Polepon, now Singkep.

NOTES

[1] *Page* 82. Polepaniang or Mapor.

[2] *Page* 82. Pole Candore, off the mouths of the Me-kong.

[1] *Page* 83. Champey: Cochin China.

[1] *Page* 84. Bay of Canberine: Cam Ranh ?

[2] *Page* 84. *De Haan*—the *Cock.*

[1] *Page* 85. *De Hoop*—the *Hope.*

[1] *Page* 87. *De Trou*—the *Faith.*

[2] *Page* 87. The island of Lemon: the Lema islands ?

[3] *Page* 87. Palicatten: Pulicat (on the Coramandel Coast).

[4] *Page* 87. Meaning Portuguese ships.

[1] *Page* 88. Tayowan or Taiwan, is to-day called Tainan.

[1] *Page* 89. Although the trade of Chinchu (Tsoan-Tsiu) had already moved to Amoy, the Dutch generally called the river and bay on which both these towns lay after it. The real name of the river is Kiuhang-Ici.

[2] *Page* 89. See J. H. van Linschoten's *Itinerario* (edition of the Linschoten-vereeniging, I, p. 48).

[1] *Page* 91. The Prince-flag (orange or red, white, blue) was the flag carried by the Dutch. It is also called the States flag and in reality was the emblem of the sovereign power of the Republic, i.e. the States General. In their dealings with Eastern peoples the Dutch East India Company found it expedient to emphasise the personal power possessed by the Stadtholder Prince of Orange.

[2] *Page* 91. *De Gouden Leeuw*—the *Golden Lion.*

[3] *Page* 91. Sincka-Pure: Singapore.

[1] *Page* 92. This expedition was commanded by the Chief Merchant Nieuwenroode, who was second in command under Reyertsz over the whole fleet. He sailed on this occasion in Bontekoe's ship, the *Groningen.*

[2] *Page* 92. The place was Ho-thau-soan, or Tiger Head. See Groeneveldt, *op. cit.*, p. 125.

[1] *Page* 97. From Nieuwenroode's reports (Groeneveldt, *op. cit.* p. 127) it would appear that the following exploits took place on the island of Ko-long-soe, opposite the town of Amoy.

[1] *Page* 113. See Introduction.

NOTES

[1] *Page* 114. *Het Wapen van Rotterdam* = the *Rotterdam Arms.* The text says that each lost 275 men, which seems hardly possible, since the crew of an East-Indiaman did not as a rule number much more than two hundred men.

[1] *Page* 115. The settlement of Dutch "free burghers" was encouraged by Coen, but it was never really desired by the Directors at home, who wanted the Company, through its officials, to monopolise all trade in the East.

[2] *Page* 115. The text has October 25th. This must be a misprint. See Groeneveldt, *op. cit.*, p. 226.

[3] *Page* 115. This Council of seven members, of whom Reyertsz was one, included only one of the masters of the fleet in its number; Bontekoe was not on it. See Introduction.

[1] *Page* 116. The Totok was the Commander of the imperial troops in the provinces of Hokkien (Fukien) and Tsetkang.

[1] *Page* 117. The Combon: by this word, which seems to be due to defective reading of Chinese, the Dutch indicated the governor of the province of Hokkien (Fukien), who resided at Hookchu (Foochow).

[1] *Page* 126. Our Masters: the usual term to describe the Directors of the Company.

[1] *Page* 129. For Willem Cornelisz Schouten see note to p. 71 above.

[1] *Page* 153. The "Amboina Massacre" (see Introduction) had taken place in March, 1623. On August 17th, 1624, the English Ambassador at the Hague had for the first time addressed a complain· about the affair to the States-General. On November 2nd, 1624, King James I had issued letters of reprisal against the goods and ships of the Dutch East India Company.

[1] *Page* 156. It was probably Deutel, the printer, with his zeal for the glory of Hoorn, who persuaded Bontekoe to add these particulars about Schouten. One seems to detect his peculiar style of writing in this introductory sentence.